Revised Edition

Collins

Knowledge Lighthouse

A SKILL-BASED COURSE ON GENERAL KNOWLEDGE

4

Seema Chari
Kunal Savarkar

Components of DigiSuite

Student + Teacher		Teacher-only	
a animations	**ia** activities	**g** games	**lp** lesson plans	**tn** teacher's notes
ilt instructor-led tutorials	**w** worksheets	**v** videos	**w** worksheets	**ak** answer keys
	audio			

Preface

Like the universe, knowledge, too, is limitless. No matter how much we know, there is always more to know. In the 21st century, thanks to the leaps that technology has made and continues to make, we shall have to gather knowledge throughout our lives; so much so that we have coined a new portmanteau, to describe it: 'upskilling'.

Another novelty of the third millennium is how we access and absorb knowledge. Apart from human sources (family, teachers, friends), there are the online ones (website, social media). Yet, despite all this easy availability and accessibility, it is not always easy to distinguish between real and fake, relevant and redundant, significant and inconsequential.

Knowledge Lighthouse Revised Edition is a series meant for GenZ, that is, learners born after Y2K. The series covers 'classic' general knowledge content for learners of grades 1 to 8, but lays special emphasis on skills —learning skills, literacy skills and life skills— as well as knowledge gleaned from new learnings of the past few years, from COVID-19 to sustainability, from data science to global issues in an ever-shifting, ever-ephemeral, post-information world. All the new chapters, although dealing with topics of great gravity, are presented in an age-appropriate and friendly manner so as to kindle interest and lay the foundation for more in-depth learning.

A critical component of the Knowledge Lighthouse Revised Edition books is the India content, wherein our country in all its complexity and diversity is presented through colourful, simple and exciting tasks, plus brand-new features such as state-focus, city-focus and visit-a-monument.

A particularly career-friendly inclusion in the Knowledge Lighthouse Revised Edition series is Science, technology, engineering and mathematics (STEM), the disciplines of the future, and new global issues, presented under World Today. We hope to lighten these subjects for students, by adding a little sprinkle of trivia to them.

Sustainable development is one of the key phrases of this millennium, but what does it really mean for us, especially for children? The all-new Life on Land and Climate Action chapters not only sensitise learners but also encourage direct and immediate action.

In the Skills pages, the life skills section has tasks on safety and self-awareness. Connecting the dots is the foundation of knowledge and the series has chapters based on Higher Order Thinking Skills (HOTS) and critical thinking to train young minds to see patterns, learn to eliminate or choose details and observe better.

Become a Champion Quizzer

Knowledge Lighthouse Revised Edition encourages all learners to be curious and explore the world around them. Those who observe and absorb all the time, learn from everyone and everything; they are the ones who become quizzers. Here are six rules that will help you become a champion quizzer.

1. Be curious—look around you, see everything, read everything.
2. Listen to others.
3. Seek out new experiences.
4. Learn to link events and people.
5. Do your own research and learn to spot fake news.
6. Remember, no matter how much you know, there is much more that you have yet to learn.

Now, go for it! We are sure that this series will expose a whole new generation of learners to the fun universe of general knowledge and enhance their love for learning and discovery.

~ Seema Chari and Kunal Savarkar

In this series ...

Knowledge Lighthouse tasks are thematic and linear with visual, verbal, and strategic inputs to help students solve them and acquire knowledge through a wide range of subjects and themes.

World Around Us

8 World Traditional Dresses

We can wear clothes made in different places today, thanks to trade and travel. In ma communities around the world, there are clothes for special occasions or simply for a change in weather conditions.

Look at the pictures and match them to the descriptions and the countries in which thes clothes are worn using their flags as clues. Then write the answer in the box provided. On has been done for you.

Traditional Dresses	Descriptions	Flags
1	a The elegant *traje de flamenca* is a long dress with	i

World Around Us tasks take the learners on an exciting journey across the world.

Natural World

15 Aquatic Water Pl

Aquatic plants are plants that grow in saltwater or freshwater. Submerged pla fully underwater. Emergent plants are rooted in the soil below the water body leaves and stems extend out of the water.

Match these aquatic floral plants to their descriptions.

1 Water poppy 2 Buttonbush 3 Watercress

Natural World section uncovers the magical realm of plants, animals and birds.

Climate Action

18 Wipe Away Your Footprints

Tourism is an important industry that impacts the economy of a country and shows off the best of every place to visit. However, when tourists visit these places, they often leave very ugly footprints behind.

Sustainable Development Goals sensitises learners towards sustainable development of the planet.

India Focus

19 Singing for India

Some songs make us feel proud as Indians.

Read the lines about some of these songs and fill in the blanks using words from th

1 The national anthem of India, *Jana gana mana* was written in .... and composed by ....

2 The national anthem was first sung publicly in 1911. The full version of the anthem takes .... seconds to be performed.

India Focus tasks are created to evoke a sense of wonder and pride in our nation.

Art and Entertainment

30 Superhumans

When there is chaos in the world, we need superhumans to save the planet.

Read the descriptions and match them to the names of some superhumans.

1 Peter Parker spins his webs across New York City and saves it from the clutches of Doctor Octopus.

2 Steve Rodgers becomes a super soldier, the leader of the Avengers.

a Iron Man

b Captain Marvel

Art and Entertainment tasks celebrate artists, artworks, paintings, movies, awards and achievements.

Sports

40 Sporting Terms

Write the names of the sports with which these terms are associated.

1 backstroke butterfly freestyle lap

2 dismount vault balance beam floor exercise

3 shaft arrowhead arm guard target point

Sports section provides rules and records related to different sports.

Language and Literature

43 Which Book is That?

Read the clues and select the correct words to complete the names of these books. Match the authors to the books by writing the correct letters in the boxes.

1 Every night, Charlie listens to Grandpa Joe tell stories about Mr Willy Wonka.
Charlie and the .... *Soap/Chocolate Factory*

2 Jerusha Abbott was brought up at an old-fashioned orphanage. The children were wholly dependent on charity.
Daddy-Long .... *-Legs/Hair*

Language and Literature tasks present vocabulary and etymology in a fun way.

World Today

10 A COVID-19 P

The world changed in many ways thanks to the COVID-19 pandemic.

Here is a crossword whose clues lead to terms that we have all heard in the la

Word Today introduces the learner to the COVID and post-COVID world.

Whiz fact

The Incredibles is a film series about superheroes who have been ordere superpowers, but are finally forced to use them to, what else, but save the w

52

Whiz Fact is a spin-off fact about each topic or theme.

General Science

3 Visiting the Doctor

Use the clues to complete the crossword about things we can see at a doctor's clinic.

General Science highlights some scientific achievements and provides facts for others.

Whiz quiz

In which of these countries in southeast Asia is a conical hat called *non la* worn?

a Malaysia b Indonesia c Vietnam

Whiz Quiz are fun activities that encourage self-learning.

21st Century Skills

21st century skills are necessary to succeed in the Age of Information. These skills are divided into three main sets, namely, learning skills, literacy skills and life skills.

Learning Skills

- Critical Thinking and HOTS
- Creativity
- Collaboration
- Communication

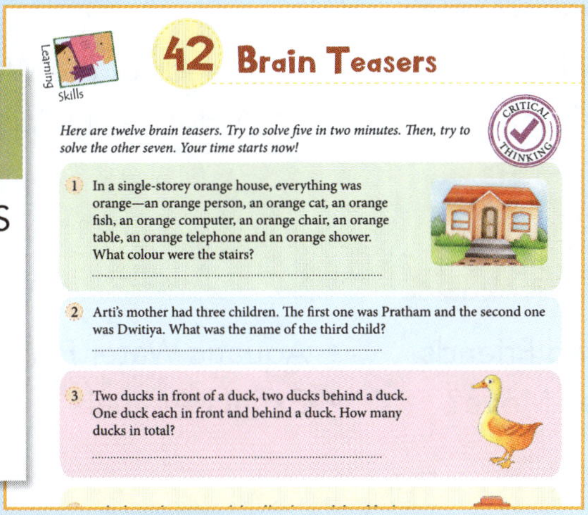

Learning Skills

42 Brain Teasers

Here are twelve brain teasers. Try to solve five in two minutes. Then, try to solve the other seven. Your time starts now!

1. In a single-storey orange house, everything was orange—an orange person, an orange cat, an orange fish, an orange computer, an orange chair, an orange table, an orange telephone and an orange shower. What colour were the stairs?
2. Arti's mother had three children. The first one was Pratham and the second one was Dwitiya. What was the name of the third child?
3. Two ducks in front of a duck, two ducks behind a duck. One duck each in front and behind a duck. How many ducks in total?

Literacy Skills

- Technology
- Information
- Media
- Financial Literacy
- Data Handling

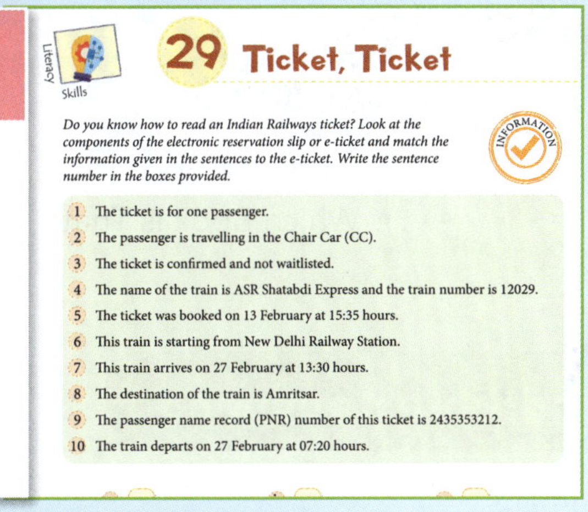

Literacy Skills

29 Ticket, Ticket

Do you know how to read an Indian Railways ticket? Look at the components of the electronic reservation slip or e-ticket and match the information given in the sentences to the e-ticket. Write the sentence number in the boxes provided.

1. The ticket is for one passenger.
2. The passenger is travelling in the Chair Car (CC).
3. The ticket is confirmed and not waitlisted.
4. The name of the train is ASR Shatabdi Express and the train number is 12029.
5. The ticket was booked on 13 February at 15:35 hours.
6. This train is starting from New Delhi Railway Station.
7. This train arrives on 27 February at 13:30 hours.
8. The destination of the train is Amritsar.
9. The passenger name record (PNR) number of this ticket is 2435353212.
10. The train departs on 27 February at 07:20 hours.

Life Skills

- Problem-solving
- Self-awareness
- Safety
- Social Skills

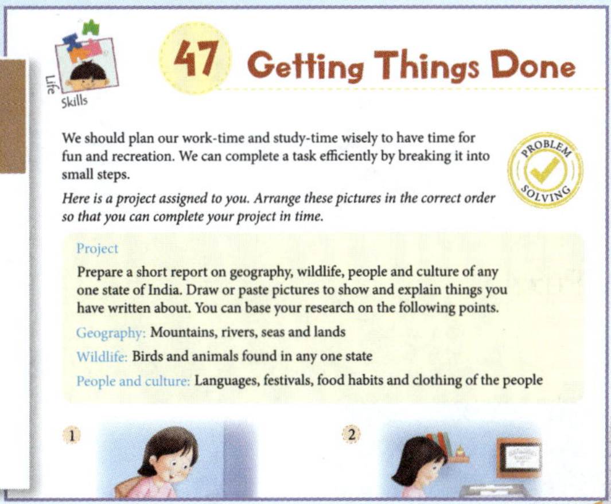

Life Skills

47 Getting Things Done

We should plan our work-time and study-time wisely to have time for fun and recreation. We can complete a task efficiently by breaking it into small steps.

Here is a project assigned to you. Arrange these pictures in the correct order so that you can complete your project in time.

Project

Prepare a short report on geography, wildlife, people and culture of any one state of India. Draw or paste pictures to show and explain things you have written about. You can base your research on the following points.

Geography: Mountains, rivers, seas and lands

Wildlife: Birds and animals found in any one state

People and culture: Languages, festivals, food habits and clothing of the people

1

2

Detailed Contents

India Focus

- India in Colours
- Enjoy the Festivities
- Great Lines
- Singing for India
- Northward Ho!
- Mountains of India
- Kolkata
- Presidents of India
- Jantar Mantar
- State Capitals of India
- Param Vir Chakra
- Percussion Instruments
- Wildlife of Northeast India

Sports

- Sporting Terms
- Equipped to Play

Sustainable Development Goals

- Wipe Away Your Footprints
- Biodegradable Things

Learning Skills

- Name Mnemonics
- Common Abbreviations
- Brain Teasers
- Word Relationships

Literacy Skills

- Using Money
- Cars and More
- Appsolutely Great
- Ticket, Ticket
- Grocery Shopping
- Measuring Things

Life Skills

- Road Signs
- Etiquette
- Safety First
- Getting Things Done

Contents

India Focus

1 India in Colours

Many places and things connected to them in India have nicknames. Here are some of them. They are all names of colours.

Fill in the blanks using the words from the help box.

1. Jaipur is known as the .... Maharaja Jai Singh II had the city walls and buildings painted a rosy brick colour to welcome the Prince of Wales.

2. Jodhpur is known as the .... The houses in the old city are painted a bluish colour to keep them cool.

3. The Nilgiris are known as the .... The neelakurinji flower blooms every twelve years and gives the hilly slopes a brilliant blue-violet colour.

4. The town of Haldighati, where a famous battle was fought, was named for its .... soil. It looks like the colour of turmeric.

5. The .... runs from Kolkata to Dhanbad, a town where coal mines are found.

6. The .... in Delhi is named after the red sandstone of which it is made.

Help box

Blue Mountains	Blue City	Black Diamond Express
Red Fort	yellow	Pink City

Whiz fact

The English word orange is derived from the Sanskrit word *nãranga*, which means an 'orange tree'.

Natural World

2 Our Feathered Friends

Read the clues and solve the rebus puzzles to find the names of these birds.

Clues	Rebus	Bird
1 A bird of prey with powerful talons and keen eyesight		 = ...
2 A large water bird with a distinct pouch under its beak	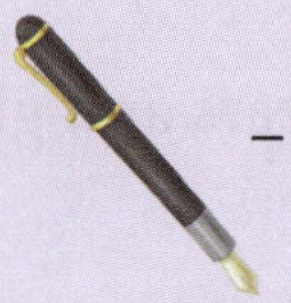 – N + L I + 	 = ...
3 A long-legged bird that flies with its neck stretched		 = ...
4 A medium-sized songbird	 +  – M – E	 = ...

5 A nocturnal bird with a large flat and hooked beak, it gapes like the animal it is named after.

 + 

= ....

6 A bird with a long and thin neck which makes it look like a snake

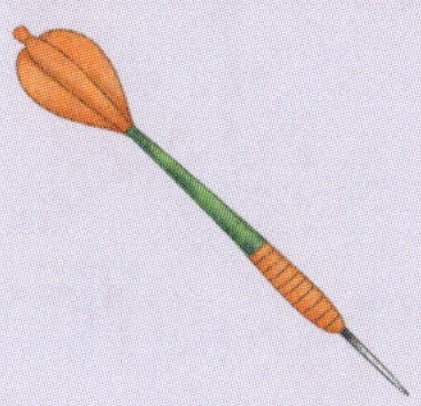 + ER

= ....

7 A kind of vulture, it is one of the largest flying land birds.

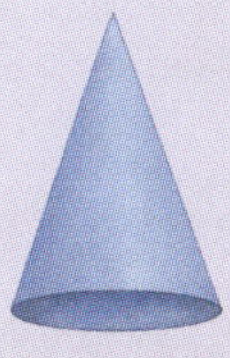 – E +  – O

= ....

8 The second-tallest living bird, it is Australia's largest native bird.

E +  – S I C

= ....

Whiz fact

Weaver birds make interesting nests shaped like cans with a narrow entrance at the bottom. This makes it difficult for predators to enter the nest and eat their eggs or young ones.

General Science

3 Visiting the Doctor

Use the clues to solve the crossword about things we can see at a doctor's clinic.

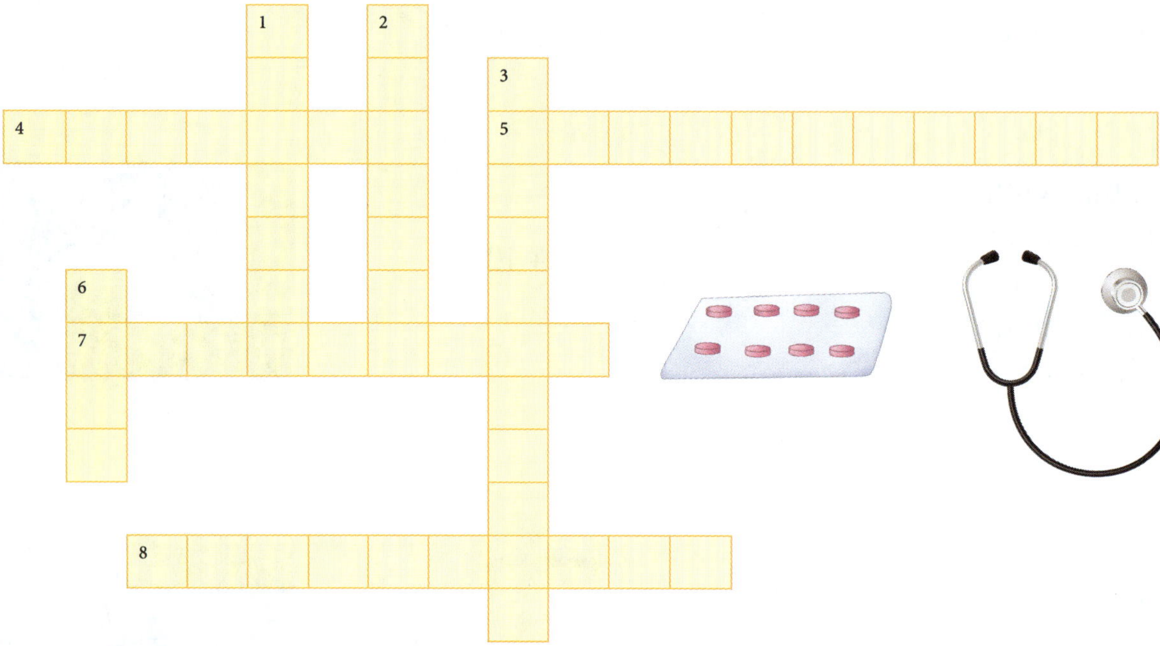

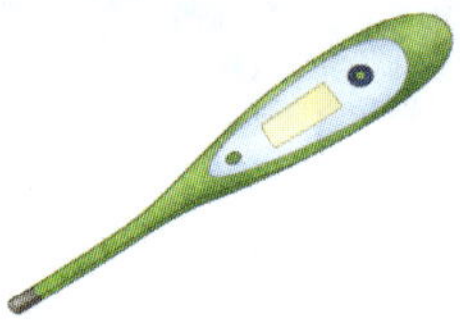

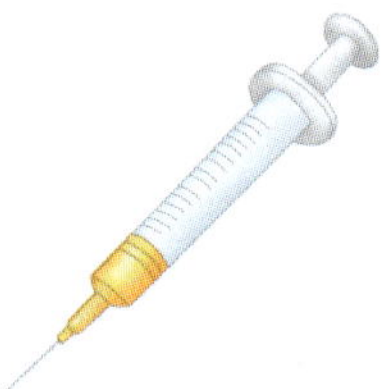

Across

4. A small tube with a thin hollow needle at the end
5. An instrument doctors use for measuring body temperature
7. When a doctor or a nurse puts medicine into our body using a device with a needle
8. A cream that helps to prevent infection in wounds

Down

1. A strip of cloth tied around a part of the body that has been hurt
2. A person who sells medicines
3. An instrument that a doctor uses to listen to somebody's heart and breathing
6. A small flat round piece of medicine that we swallow without chewing.

Language and Literature

4 Back and Forth

A palindrome is a word that reads the same backwards and forwards. Numbers, phrases and even sentences can be palindromes. Spaces and punctuation between the words are allowed. For example, the word 'refer' is a palindrome because it reads the same, whether you read it forwards or backwards.

Read the clues to find some palindromes and write them in the blanks provided.

1

A three-letter-word that means 'mother'...

2

Another word for midday
....

3

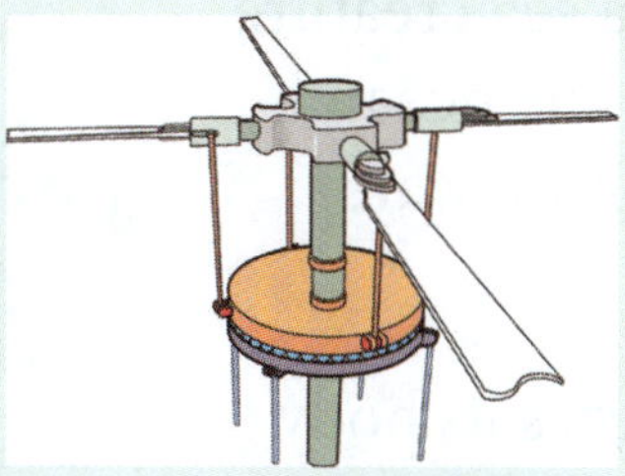

Four long blades which rotate and lift a helicopter off the ground ....

4

A narrow boat that moves with a double-bladed paddle
....

5

One of a series of stages in a game
....

6

A three-letter word used to express surprise ....

Whiz fact

The longest palindrome is believed to be the Finnish word *saippuakivikauppias*, which means 'soapstone vendor'.

Natural World

5 How Do They Move?

Fill in the blanks with names of correct sea creatures.

Penguin

Jellyfish

Sea turtle

Octopus

1. A .... uses its fins to move through water, maintain balance and change direction.
2. A .... is a flightless bird that uses its flippers to swim in water.
3. A .... uses its short, stubby wing-like fins to swim in water.
4. A .... uses its webbed feet to jump on land and swim in water.
5. The .... is a sea creature with eight limbs that can walk on the ocean floor. Sometimes, it moves by sucking water and pushing it out.
6. A .... squeezes its body in order to push jets of water from the bottom of its body to move forward.
7. A .... thrusts its body from side to side in an S-shaped movement to push itself forward.
8. A .... moves its whole body in a wave-like motion to move through water.

Snake

Fish

Stingray

Frog

Whiz fact

The Portuguese man o' war is a jellyfish-like creature which does not really swim. It has a bladder which inflates and deflates depending on whether it wants to be closer to or farther away from the sea's surface.

6 Gender Nouns

It's been raining for 40 days and the animal pairs need to board Noah's Ark lest they drown.

Read the names of animals and write their gender names with the help of the clues and words from the help box.

Animals	Female	Male
1 Donkey	a	i Jack
2 Bear	b Sow	ii ....
3 Chicken	c	iii ....
4 Camel	d	iv Bull
5 Deer	e Doe	v ....
6 Fox	f	vi ....
7 Goose	g	vii ....
8 Goat	h Nanny	viii ....
9 Horse	i Mare	ix ....
10 Sheep	j	x ....
11 Swan	k	xi Cob
12 Bee	l	xii Drone

Help box

Stallion	Vixen	Cow	Jenny	Queen	Buck	Ewe	Rooster
Goose	Billy	Dog	Pen	Ram	Hen	Boar	Gander

Whiz fact

In ant and bee colonies, only one female is the queen and others are called workers or drones. This is the origin of the phrase 'to be the queen bee', meaning to get others to do as you wish.

Natural World

7 Big Cats

There are many species of cats, but some are called big cats. All big cats are carnivores. They are found in North America, South America, Africa and Asia.

Read the clues and write the names of some big cats in the crossword puzzle. The first letter of each answer has been given for you.

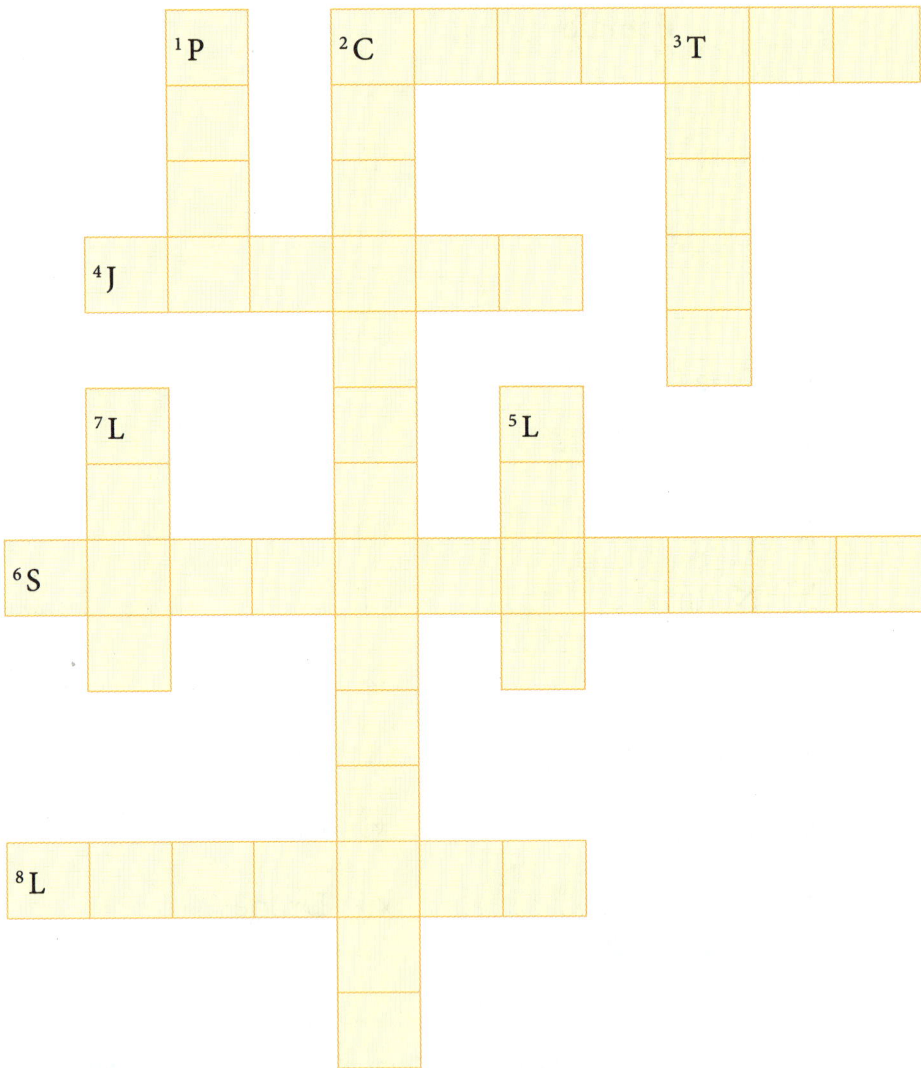

Whiz fact

The cat family is also called the feline family. Most members of this family are patterned with spots, stripes or rosettes on their body. The rusty-spotted cat is its smallest member.

Across

2 The fastest land animal, it runs at a speed of nearly 113 km per hour.

4 The national animal of Guyana, it has yellowish-brown fur with black rings and spots.

6 A big cat that lives in the cold deserts of Asia, it is often called 'ghost of the mountain' because it is rarely seen.

8 It is a big cat with dark spots called rosettes, which create a beautiful pattern against its light fur.

Down

1 A big cat that is also known as mountain lion or cougar, it has brownish-grey fur.

2 A big cat which is more at home on trees than on the ground, it has the longest canine teeth of any living feline.

3 The largest member of the cat family, it is known by its stripes.

5 It is the only big cat with a mane.

7 It is a big cat with a short tail and large pointy ears.

World Around Us

8 World Traditional Dresses

We can wear clothes made in different places today, thanks to trade and travel. In many communities around the world, there are clothes for special occasions or simply for a change in weather conditions.

Look at the pictures and match them to the descriptions and the countries in which these clothes are worn using their flags as clues. Then write the answer in the box provided. One has been done for you.

Traditional Dresses	Descriptions	Flags	
1 	a The elegant *traje de flamenca* is a long dress with ruffles worn by women in Andalusia.	i  Japan	1 c ii
2 	b The kimono is a wraparound dress worn with a sash.	ii  Scotland	
3 	c The kilt is a kind of skirt worn by men.	iii  Bhutan	
4 	d The *gho* is a dress worn by men in a country in the Himalayan region.	iv  Spain	

5		e	The *sarafan* is a long dress worn by women in a transcontinental country located in Europe and Asia.	v	 Mexico
6		f	The sari is a single length of fabric that can be draped in dozens of different ways.	vi	 Russia
7		g	The *huipil* is a colourful embroidered loose-fitting tunic worn by indigenous women of Central America.	vii	 South Korea
8		h	The *hanbok* is an outfit consisting of a fitted blouse and a flared skirt.	viii	 India

Whiz quiz

In which of these countries in southeast Asia is a conical hat called *non la* worn?

a Malaysia   b Indonesia   c Vietnam

Whiz fact

The *kanga* is a colourful outfit worn in different countries around the African Great Lakes. The earliest patterns made on the *kanga* resembled the speckled plumage of a bird called Guinea fowl.

Literacy Skills

9 Using Money

Seema carried the same amount of money in her wallet every day from January through March.

Read the purchases she made and write the values of notes and coins she used for payments. On every purchase, Seema paid exact change. One has been done for you.

Purchases

2 January

1 Seema bought a bouquet of flowers for ₹220.

Notes ₹200, ₹20 Coins 0

14 January

2 Seema bought a birthday gift for ₹572.

Notes .... Coins ....

22 January

3 Seema visited a dentist's clinic. She paid ₹800 as the dentist's fee.

Notes .... Coins ....

5 February

4 Seema bought a bedcover for ₹2,500 for her parents.

Notes .... Coins ....

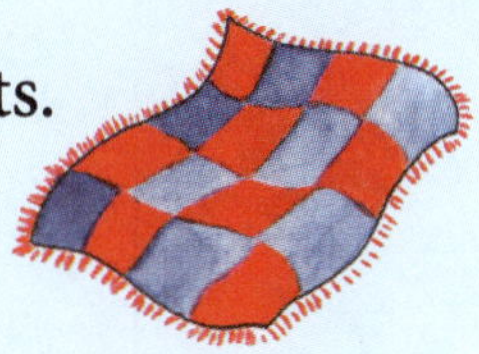

16 February

5 Seema bought a box of pencils for ₹22.

Notes .... Coins ....

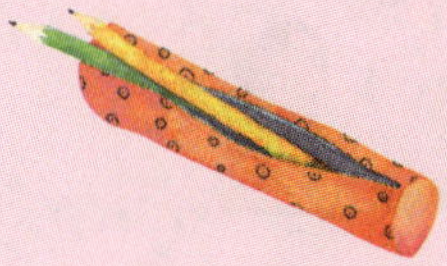

20 March

6 Seema went to a restaurant for dinner and paid a bill of ₹2,110.

Notes .... Coins ....

Whiz quiz

Which new banknote issued by the Reserve Bank of India does not have a picture of a monument on the reverse side?

....

....

....

10 A COVID-19 Puzzle

The world changed in many ways thanks to the COVID-19 pandemic.

Here is a crossword whose clues lead to terms that we have all heard in the last three years.

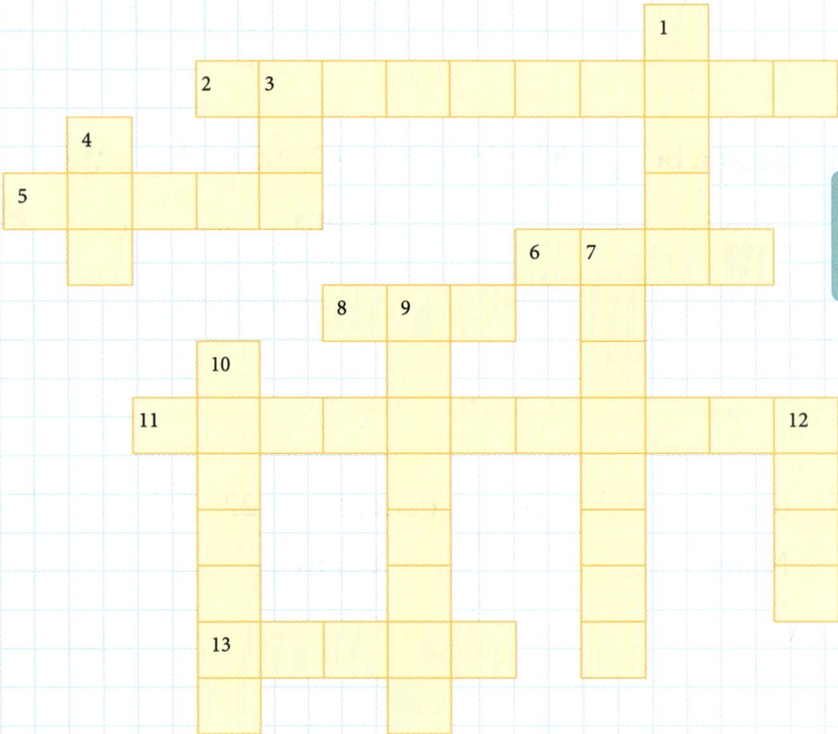

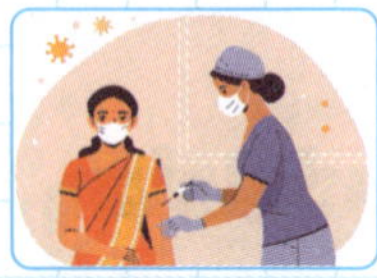

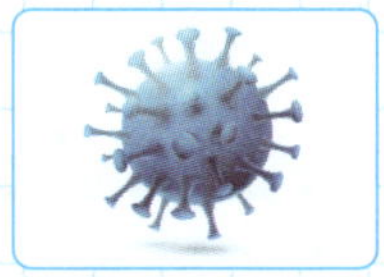

Across

2 A period during which a person stays isolated (10)

5 The country where the first cases were recorded (5)

6 Wearing this on your face reduces your chances of spreading COVID (4)

8 Short form for a special dress worn by health workers (3)

11 Full name for the organism that causes COVID (11)

13 This country set the record for most vaccinations in a day (5)

Down

1 COVID is caused by this microscopic organism (5)

3 This country recorded the greatest number of COVID cases (3)

4 The UN body which is concerned with global health (3)

7 The body produces this protein to fight COVID (8)

9 The name given to the global outbreak of a disease (8)

10 The first vaccine to be developed in India (7)

12 A plastic device with a soft end used to collect nasal samples (4)

11 Road Signs

Life Skills

Road signs keep the roads safe for pedestrians and drivers. They are of three types—circular, triangular and rectangular.

Circular signs are compulsory signs that everyone must follow.

Triangular signs are cautionary signs to warn people about unsafe conditions on the road.

Rectangular signs are informatory signs that show directions and distances of places.

Look at the signs and write what they mean using words or phrases from help box.

1 

....

2 

....

3 

....

4 

....

5 

....

6 

....

7 

....

8 

....

Help box

Speed breaker ahead | Pedestrian crossing prohibited | Zebra crossing | Directions | No U turn | Narrow road ahead | No left turn | Airport ahead

Whiz fact

The stop sign is the only eight-sided sign. It asks drivers to stop.

12 Our Neighbour, China

China is India's largest neighbour. It is also one of the few countries that is larger than India, and the only country to have a larger population than India.

Fill in the blanks with the help of the clues and the words from help box to know more about China.

1 These long thick strings made of rice are boiled or fried and eaten with a sauce in China.

....

2 This powerful creature from the Chinese mythology is often linked to the Emperor.

....

3 The Chinese invented this device that helped ships find directions.

....

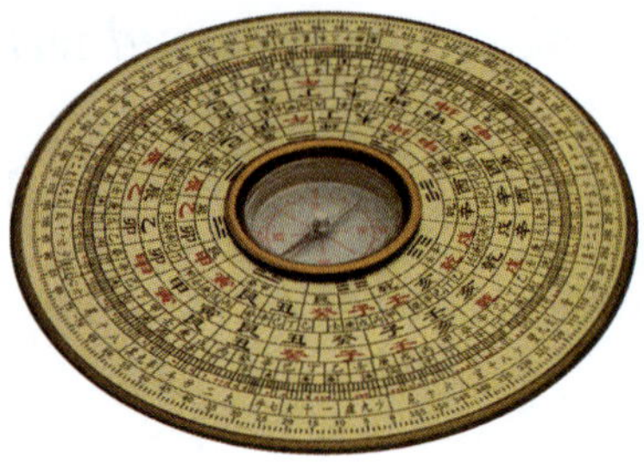

4 This is a traditional Chinese dress.

....

5 The Chinese emperor Shennong discovered it after he saw a leaf fall in boiling water.

....

6 The Chinese invented this paper basket with a small candle inside that can fly up up up.

....

7 The Chinese eat with this pair of thin sticks.

....

8 This festival that marks the end of the Chinese New Year.

....

9 It is the most important bird in Chinese legend.

....

10 Regarded a Wonder of the World, its length spans several thousand kilometres.

....

11 High-ranking official in the former imperial Chinese government were known by the name that is now the name of China's official language.

....

12 In ancient China, this flower was considered a symbol of purity.

....

Help box

Mandarin | Dragon | chopsticks | lotus | tea | Lantern Festival | noodles
sky lantern | Chinese Phoenix | cheongsam | compass | Great Wall of China

Whiz fact

Red is considered a lucky colour in Chinese culture. It is used widely during festivals like Lantern Festival, Chinese New Year and even in weddings.

India Focus

13 Enjoy the Festivities

India is a land of many festivals. Here are names of some of the festivals that are celebrated in India.

Read the clues and write the names of the festivals using words from the help box.

1 A festival celebrating the bond between brothers and sisters

....

2 A festival celebrated in April, marking the new year in Kerala

....

3 A festival marking the end of the holy month of Ramadan

....

4 The birth of Zoroaster, founder of the Parsi religion called Zoroastrianism

....

5 An Odia festival commemorating the annual visit of Lord Jagannath of Puri to the Gundicha Temple in Puri. The deity is accompanied by his sister and elder brother—all on their chariots

....

6 The birth of Krishna celebrated by re-enacting scenes from his birth and singing devotional songs in temples

....

Whiz fact

Makar Sankranti is also called *Thai Pongal* in Tamil Nadu and *Magh Bihu* in Assam.

7 The birth of Guru Nanak, the first Sikh Guru and the founder of Sikhism

....

8 The beginning of the Telugu and Kannada new years (The festival is called Gudi Padwa in Maharashtra)

....

9 A festival celebrating the birthday of the founder of Jainism

....

10 The birth of Prophet Muhammad, the founder of Islam

....

11 The birth of Jesus Christ in Bethlehem

....

12 A festival marking the harvest season and the end of winter in Punjab

....

13 Shivaratri, as celebrated by the people of Jammu and Kashmir

....

Help box

Eid-ul-Fitr	Khordad Sal	Rath Yatra	Janamashtami	Bhai Dooj
Gurpurab	Herath	Ugadi	Mahavir Jayanti	Vishu
	Milad-un-Nabi	Lohri	Christmas	

14 Name Mnemonics

A mnemonic helps us remember information easily. There are many types of mnemonics.

CREATIVITY

Read these mnemonics and find out what they stand for using words from the help box.

1 My Very Excited Mother Just Served Us Noodles

The eight .... of the solar system are Mercury, Venus, Earth, Mars, Jupiter, Saturn, Uranus and Neptune.

2 Super Man Helps Every One

The .... of North America from west to east are Superior, Michigan, Huron, Erie and Ontario.

3 Lazy Cats Do not Move

The .... in multiples of 10 are L = 50, C = 100, D = 500 and M = 1000.

4 Big Gorillas Eat Hotdogs Not Cold Pizza

The seven countries of .... are Belize, Guatemala, El Salvador, Honduras, Nicaragua, Costa Rica and Panama

5 Prime Ministers Cannot Eat Any Nachos

The time zones of .... from west to eastare Pacific, Mountain, Central, Eastern, Atlantic and Newfoundland.

6 No Soup For Russia

Northern .... countries from west to east are Norway, Sweden, Finland and Russia.

7 Incredibly Slimy Cockroach Bit My Aunt

The countries around the .... are Italy, Slovenia, Bosnia and Herzegovina, Montenegro and Albania.

Help box

Great Lakes | Canada | planets | Central America | Roman numerals | European | Adriatic Sea

Whiz quiz

Make a mnemonic for the union territories of India.

....

....

....

....

....

Whiz fact

A mnemonic for remembering the steps for treating a sprain is the word 'rice'.

Rest the sprained part

Ice the sprained area

Compress with a bandage

Elevate the sprained part

Natural World

15 Aquatic Water Plants

Aquatic plants are plants that grow in saltwater or freshwater. Submerged plants grow fully underwater. Emergent plants are rooted in the soil below the water body, but their leaves and stems extend out of the water.

Match these aquatic floral plants to their descriptions by writing the correct letter in the boxes given.

1 

Water poppy

2 

Buttonbush

3 

Watercress

4 

Cardinal flower

5 

Water hyacinth

a A common North American shrub having dense, round clusters of small hairy, white flowers.

b A floating aquatic plant with swollen leafstalks, it forms dense masses in rivers and ponds.

c This plant grows in the wetlands. Its bright-red flowers grow at the end of long stems.

d This plant has lemon-yellow coloured flowers with red-brown centres and dark green, round leaves.

e This small plant with white flowers grows in streams and pools. Its leaves taste hot and are eaten raw in salads.

6 

Lizard's tail

7 

Japanese iris

8 

Pickerelweed

9 

Water hawthorn

10 

Water lily

f A North American freshwater plant having arrow-shaped leaves and purple flowers, it shares its name with a fish.

g An ornamental plant with large flat leaves and colourful cup-shaped flowers, it floats on the surface of lakes and rivers.

h This plant has long shiny leaves and produces tiny, tube-like Y-shaped blue flowers on spikes.

i This plant has dark green leaves and showy clusters of blue or purple, broad trumpet-shaped flowers.

j The aquatic plant has a bottle-brush spike of white flowers. The flower spike arches above the leaves of the plant.

Whiz quiz

Find out why most aquatic plants have spongy leaves and stems.

Whiz fact

Submerged plants, especially those that grow in deep oceans, do not get much sunlight, yet they undergo photosynthesis.

India Focus

16 Great Lines

The leaders of India said some great lines or slogans that are still famous.

Complete each slogan using words from the help box. The meanings of the slogans and names of the leader associated with each slogan are already given.

Slogans	Meanings	Who Said It?
1 *Jai*	Victory to India!	 Subhas Chandra Bose
2 *Satyameva*	Truth alone triumphs.	 Madan Mohan Malviya
3 *Inquilab*	Long live the revolution!	 Bhagat Singh
4 *Vande*	Hail my motherland!	 Bankim Chandra Chattopadhyay
5 *Jai Jawaan Jai*	Victory to the soldier, Victory to the farmer!	 Lal Bahadur Shastri

Help box

Kisaan *Zindabad* *Hind* *Mataram* *Jayate*

Whiz fact

The national motto of India, *Satyameva Jayate*, which translates to 'Truth alone triumphs', is a very old saying. It is inscribed on the base of India's national emblem. One can read it in Sanskrit on all banknotes of India.

17 Etiquette

SOCIAL SKILLS

It is important to behave politely in a particular situation. This is called etiquette.

Match the lines to the pictures and tick those that show people with good etiquette.

1 Stand calmly in a queue while waiting.

2 Don't cover your mouth while yawning, coughing or sneezing.

3 Offer your seat to senior citizens.

4 Try to get inside a lift before people can exit.

5 Walk up an escalator that is moving down.

6 Scold the waiter if you do not like your food.

a  ☐

b  ☐

c  ☐

d  ☐

e  ☐

f  ☐

Whiz fact

The word 'etiquette' is derived from French, in which it means 'tag' or 'label'. Etiquette has no plural form.

Climate Action

18 Wipe Away Your Footprints

Tourism is an important industry that impacts the economy of a country and shows off the best of every place to visit. However, when tourists visit these places, they often leave very ugly footprints behind.

Whiz fact

If your travels in the outdoors include places where there might be bees or wasps, avoid bright colours such as yellow or blue, or dark colours such as red or purple, and do not wear strong perfume. Also avoid tight-fitting clothing or fabrics that might make you sweat a lot. Bees and wasps are attracted to strong colours and scents. Loose white clothing in cool fabrics is best to keep you from getting stung!

Read these tourist actions. If they are good for the planet, colour the footprints green. If they are bad for the planet, colour the footprint red.

Tourist Actions	Footprints
1 Tourists who carry their biodegradable waste like fruit peel, leftover bread and cake crumbs	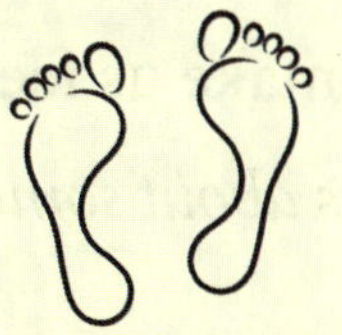
2 Tourists who bury wrappers, packets and paper napkins in the ground	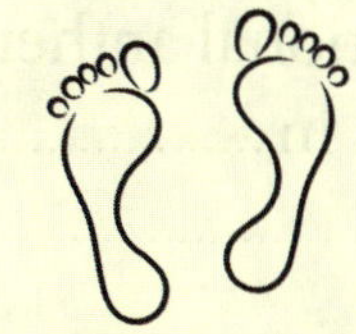
3 Tourists who pick wildflowers	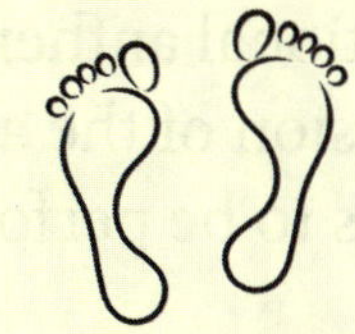
4 Tourists who keep their voice low in a forest as the noise could disturb the animals living in the forest.	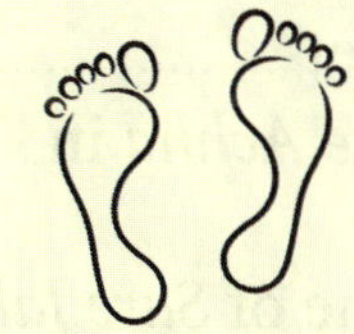
5 Tourists who carve their names on the bark of trees	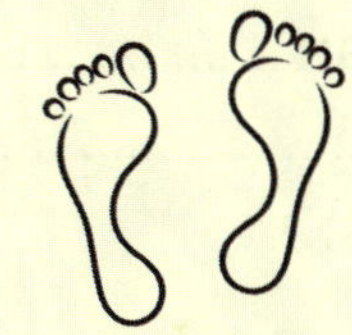
6 Tourists who go off established trails to wander down 'paths not taken'	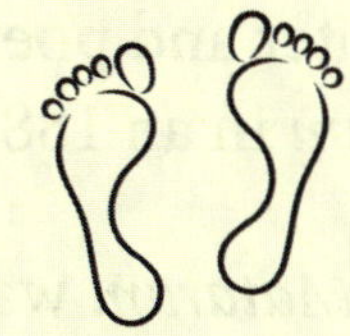
7 Tourists who wear camouflage clothing to merge in the surroundings.	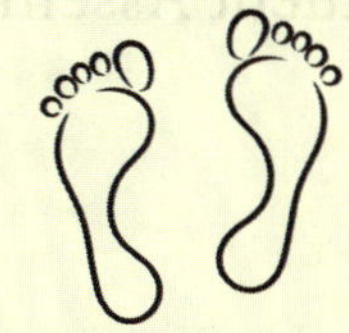
8 Tourists who wash their clothes in forest streams	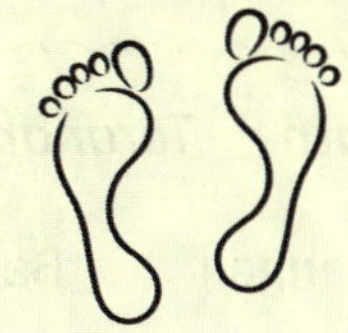

19 Singing for India

Some songs make us feel proud as Indians.

Read the lines about some of these songs and fill in the blanks using words from the help box.

1. The national anthem of India, *Jana gana mana* was written in .... and composed by ....

2. The national anthem was first sung publicly in 1911. The full version of the anthem takes .... seconds to be performed.

3. The poet .... composed the song *Sare Jahan se Achha* in ....in the year 1904.

4. The tune of *Sare Jahan se Achha* was composed by the great musician .... The song is also called .... , which means an 'Anthem of Indians'.

5. The writer and poet .... wrote *Vande Mataram* in an 1881 novel called ....

6. *Vande Mataram* was adopted as the national song by the Constituent Assembly of India in ....

Help box

Anandamath | *Taranah-e-Hindi* | Pandit Ravi Shankar | 52 | Urdu | Rabindranath Tagore | Bengali | Bankim Chandra Chattopadhyay | Muhammad Iqbal | 1950

Whiz fact

The National Anthem of Bangladesh is called *Amar Shonar Bangla*. It was composed by Rabindranath Tagore.

20 Once Upon a Time

Read the opening lines of some famous books and write the names of the books using the help box.

1 In an old house in Paris that was covered with vines lived twelve little girls in two straight lines.

....

2 First of all, let me get something straight: this is a JOURNAL, not a diary.

....

3 Dorothy lived in the midst of the great Kansas prairies, with Uncle Henry, who was a farmer, and Aunt Em, who was the farmer's wife.

....

4 It's a funny thing about mothers and fathers.

....

5 The sun did not shine.
It was too wet to play.
So we sat in the house
All that cold, cold wet day.

....

6 Mr and Mrs Dursley, of number four, Privet Drive, were proud to say that they were perfectly normal, thank you very much.

....

7 Look, I didn't want to be a half-blood.

....

Help box

Diary of a Wimpy Kid | *Madeline* | *Matilda* | *The Wizard of Oz* | *Harry Potter and the Philosopher's Stone* | *Cat in the Hat* | *The Lightening Thief*

Whiz fact

The first sentence of L M Montgomery's *Anne of the Green Gables* has 148 words!

Literacy Skills

21 Cars and More

Read the names of these car brands and their descriptions to match with the logos.

1 Fiat	The four letters of its name	a 
2 Toyota	Two ovals that make up a T	b 
3 Suzuki	A stylised S	c 
4 Honda	A plump and squat H	d 
5 Volkswagen	One letter inside another	e 
6 Hyundai	A slanting H	f 

7 Audi	Four rings	g 
8 Volvo	Name written in print	h 
9 Renault	A diamond	i 
10 Ferrari	A prancing horse	j 
11 Jaguar	An animal's face or a leaping animal	k 
12 Chevrolet	Plus sign	l 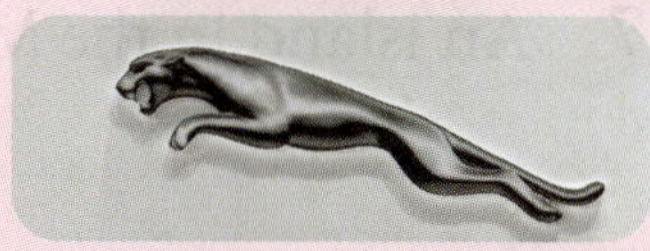
13 Ford	Name written in running hand	m 

Whiz fact

Henry Ford was the first person to manufacture automobiles on a mass scale in a factory by developing the assembly line technique of mass production.

22 Islands of the World

An island is a piece of land completely surrounded by water. Islands are mostly found in seas and oceans, but they can also be found in rivers and lakes.

Read the lines and write the names of these islands using words from the help box.

1 Two islands of Indonesia

.... and ....

2 Japan's biggest island

....

3 An island in the Caribbean Sea

....

4 A large island in the Indian Ocean

....

5 An island in the Atlantic Ocean, west of Great Britain

....

6 An island immediately south of India

....

7 An island in the Mediterranean Sea

....

8 An island to the east of mainland China

....

Help box

Taiwan	Sri Lanka	Madagascar	Borneo	Honshu
Ireland	Sumatra	Cyprus	Jamaica	

Whiz fact

Treasure Island, *Robinson Crusoe* and *The Swiss Family Robinson* are novels in which most of the story takes place on an island.

Literacy Skills

23 Appsolutely Great

TECHNOLOGY

Mobile phones and smartphones have many apps.

Read the statements and write the names of the apps using the images as clues.

1. This messaging and media sharing app has a "ghostly" appearance on a yellow background.

   ....

2. This social audio app has a waving hand as its logo.

   ....

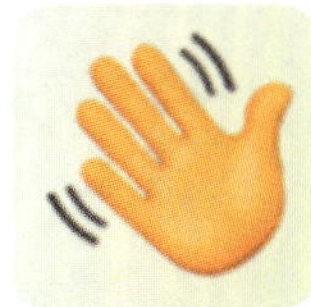

3. This browser app has a circle with red, green and yellow parts and a small blue circle at the centre.

   ....

4. This app has a little blue bird with a pointy beak.

   ....

5. This app helps us find a place. It has a green, red and grey map with a pin and the letter G on it.

   ....

6. This video app has a red box with a white play symbol in it.

   ....

Whiz fact

Koo is an Indian microblogging and social networking service, which was first launched in 2019 in Kannada! Co-founded by entrepreneurs Aprameya Radhakrishna and Mayank Bidawatka, it won the government's Atmanirbhar App Innovation Challenge.

India Focus

24 Northward Ho!

North India is known for its crafts and many wonderful places.

Read the descriptions and write the names of state or union territory to which these tourist destinations and crafts belong using names from the help box. The names from the help box may be used more than once.

Tourist Destinations

1

The Golden Temple is in Amritsar, close to the India-Pakistan border.

....

3

Naini Lake is in the Kumaon region, in the lap of the Himalayas.

....

5

Fatehpur Sikri is close to Agra.

....

Crafts

2

Garhwal paintings are made in the Garhwal Himalayas, near India's border with Nepal.

....

4

The monasteries of Dharamshala are in the Kangra district. Dharamshala's most famous resident is the Dalai Lama.

....

6

Papier mâché is a special craft of India's northernmost union territory.

....

7

Gold and silver embroidery on silk is a speciality of sarees from Banaras and nearby towns.

....

8

Woollen shawls with colourful motifs are specially woven in the Kullu Valley.

....

9

Zanskar Valley is close to Tibet.

....

10

Phulkari embroidery is popular in cities like Patiala, Jalandhar, Nabha and Ludhiana.

....

Help box

Jammu and Kashmir | Himachal Pradesh | Punjab | Uttarakhand | Uttar Pradesh | Ladakh

Whiz quiz

Which state in north India is known as the 'land of five rivers'?

Whiz fact

Houseboats made of wood are moored along the shore of the Dal Lake in Srinagar, Jammu and Kashmir. These are homes of different sizes, with bedrooms, bathrooms, a living room and a kitchen.

Natural World

25 Extinct Animals

These animals that once roamed the Earth in large numbers are extinct because of hunting and destruction of their habitat.

Read the descriptions and write the names of these extinct animals. The missing letters in their names are the 26 letters of the alphabet. Each is used only once in the chapter.

1 A striking animal, it was a half-zebra and half-horse and got its name from the sound it made.

.... A G G A

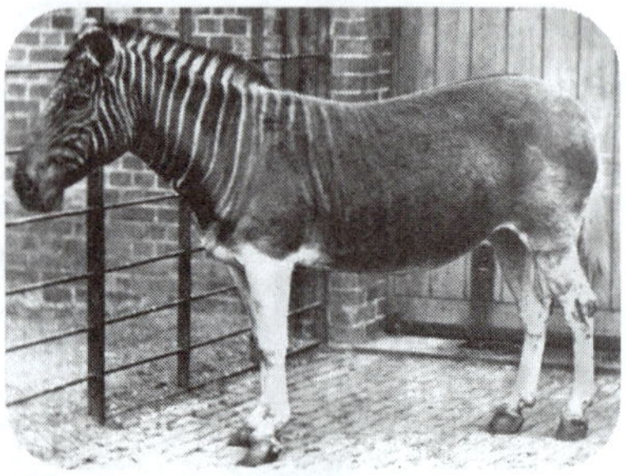

2 This huge species of flightless bird native to New Zealand grew taller than the elephants of today.

.... O A

3 Despite its name, it looked more like a tiger with short powerful limbs.

SA .... RE-TOOT .... ED CAT

4 This animal with a silvery fur was one of the heaviest and largest animals of its type in the country where it lived.

ME .... CAN GRI .... ZLY BEAR

5 The last known bird of this species died in the wild around 1900 and by 1914 the last captive bird died.

PA .... SENGER .... IGEO ....

6 This huge, plant-eating sea mammal was hunted to extinction within three decades of its discovery.

STE .... LER 'S SEA .... OW

7 This big cat lived on the Sunda Islands of Indonesia.

JA .... AN .... IGER

8 This flightless bird resembled the penguin, but it had a heavy hooked beak.

.... REAT AUK

9 This flightless bird inhabited Mauritius.

DO .... O

10 This elephant-like creature had long tusks and was covered in black, brown and ginger fur.

.... OOLL .... M .... MM .... TH

11 This giant deer could grow to a height of 7 feet and weigh up to 700 kilograms.

I .... ISH EL ....

12 This animal has shrines dedicated to it because it is regarded as a messenger of the spirits.

.... APAN .... SE HONSHU WOL ....

Whiz fact

The last captive thylacine or 'Tasmanian Tiger', often referred to as Benjamin, lived at Hobart Zoo, where it died of cold in 1936 because its cage was not protected against the extreme weather.

India Focus

26 Mountains of India

Mountains are tall and steep chunks of land. Groups of mountains are called chains or ranges. India has many mountain ranges.

Look at the map, read the clues and write the names of the mountain ranges.

1 The chain of the tallest mountains in the world, its name means 'Land of Snow'.

....

2 The two mountain ranges that stretch along the eastern and western coasts of India.

....

3 The mountain range that divides India into two parts—north and south, its name is mentioned in the national anthem of India.

....

4 The mountain ranges that are located in the northeast of India.

....

5 This range has some of the oldest mountains in the world. It stretches across Gujarat, Rajasthan, Delhi and Haryana.

....

Whiz fact

The highest mountain in the world is Mount Everest. Tenzing Norgay and Edmund Hillary were the first people to climb it.

Interestingly, the Lukla airport in Nepal is called 'Tenzing-Hillary' airport. It is considered a starting point for Mount Everest treks.

27 Parts of a Book

Use the clues and words from the help box to solve the crossword and find out the names of different parts of a book.

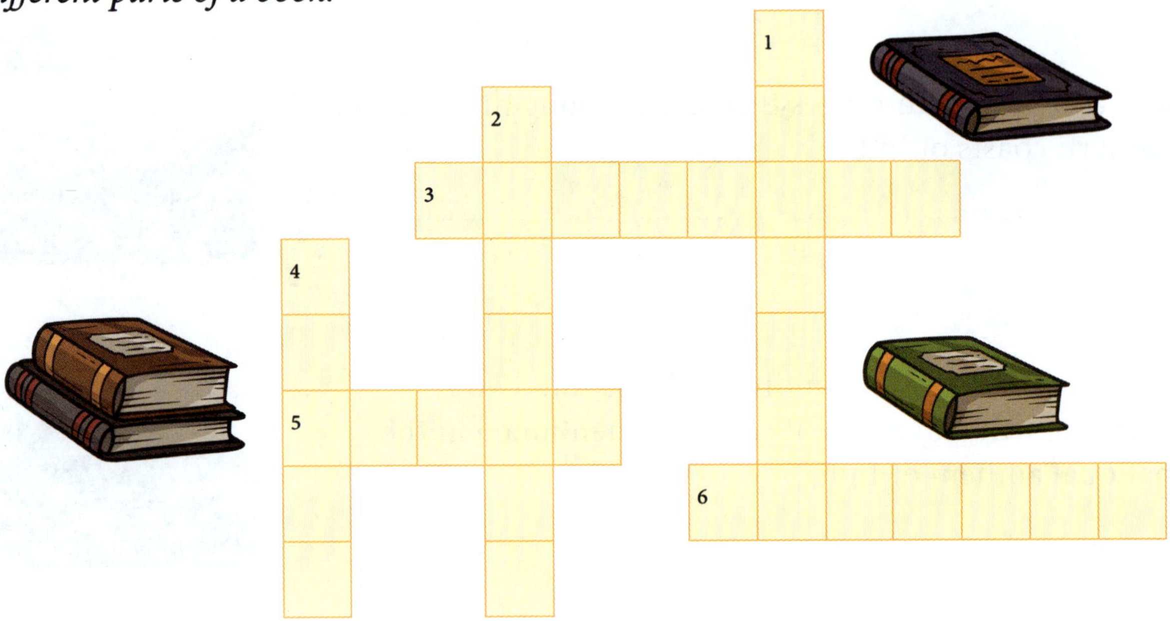

Across

3. A list of special words and their meanings
5. An alphabetical list printed at the back of a book which indicates the pages on which important topics are referred to
6. An introduction to the book that describes it in brief and explains the reason for which it was written

Down

1. Parts into which a book is divided
2. A blank page at the beginning and the end of the book
4. The backbone of the book where its title is visible when it is upright

Help box

spine preface index glossary chapter flyleaf

Whiz fact

A prologue is a speech or a section of text that introduces a book. An epilogue is a passage or speech which is added to the end of a book as a conclusion.

India Focus

28 Kolkata

The old and charming city of Kolkata is the largest city in eastern India.

Match these lines with the words to find out some facts about Kolkata.

1. The old name of Kolkata
2. Kolkata was the capital of India until this year
3. The river on which Kolkata is located
4. A famous bridge in Kolkata
5. A type of train that only Kolkata has
6. Kolkata was India's first city to have this public transport system
7. Kolkata is the capital of this state
8. A sobriquet of Kolkata

a. Tram
b. Metro system
c. West Bengal
d. City of Joy
e. Howrah
f. Calcutta
g. Hooghly
h. 1911

Whiz fact

Eden Gardens, known as the 'Colosseum of cricket', and once the world's largest capacity cricket stadium, is now the third largest after Ahmedabad's Narendra Modi Stadium and the Melbourne Cricket Ground.

Literacy Skills

29 Ticket, Ticket

Do you know how to read an Indian Railways ticket? Look at the components of the electronic reservation slip or e-ticket and match the information given in the sentences to the e-ticket. Write the sentence number in the boxes provided.

INFORMATION

1. The ticket is for one passenger.
2. The passenger is travelling in the Chair Car (CC).
3. The ticket is confirmed and not waitlisted.
4. The name of the train is ASR Shatabdi Express and the train number is 12029.
5. The ticket was booked on 13 February at 15:35 hours.
6. This train is starting from New Delhi Railway Station.
7. This train arrives on 27 February at 13:30 hours.
8. The destination of the train is Amritsar.
9. The passenger name record (PNR) number of this ticket is 2435353212.
10. The train departs on 27 February at 07:20 hours.

a ☐ b ☐ c ☐

d ☐ e ☐ f ☐

g ☐ h ☐ i ☐

j ☐

Whiz fact

As of 2022, the fastest train in India is the Vande Bharat that runs between New Delhi and Varanasi, and between New Delhi and Shri Mata Vaishno Devi Katra.

Electronic Reservation Slip

PNR No:2435353212 (a)	Train No. & Name: 12029/ASR SHTBDI EXP (b)	Quota: GENERAL (GN)
Transaction ID: 100003207361888	Date of Time Of Booking: 13-Feb-2022 15:35:37 HRS (c)	Class: CHAIR CAR (CC) (d)
From: NEW DELHI (NDLS) (e)	Date Of Journey : 27-Feb-2022	To: AMRITSAR JN (ASR) (f)
Boarding At: NEW DELHI (NDLS)	Date Of Boarding: 27-Feb-2022	Scheduled Departure: 27-Feb-2022 07:20* (i)
Resv, Upto: AMRITSAR JN (ASR)	Scheduled Arrival: 27-Feb-2022 13:30* (h)	Adult: 1 Child: 0 (g)
Passenger Mobile No: 9717892713		Distance: 448KM
Passenger Address	D-191, 1ST FLOOR SAROJINI NAGAR-2, Sarojini Nagar S.O, South Delhi, Delhi-110023	

FARE DETAILS:

Ticket Fare*	₹2160.0	Rupee Two Thousand One Hundred sixty and Zero Paisa
Catering Charges (Incl. of GST) #	₹375.0	Rupee Three Hundred Seventy Five and Zero Paisa
IRCTC Convenience Fee (Incl. of GST)#	₹23.6	Rupee Twenty Three and Sixty Paisa
Total Fare (all inclusive)	₹2558.6	Rupee Two Thousand Five Hundred Fifty Eight and Sixty Paisa

** Inclusive of GST - ₹102.72 Only

Conveniene Fee per e-ticket irrespective of number of passengers on the ticket.

PASSENGER DETAILS:

SI NO.	Name	Age	Sex	Food Chocie	Booking Status	Current Status (j)
1.	KIRTY LABRA	25	Female	VEG	CNF/C2/37/WINDOW SIDE	CNF/C2/37/WINDOW SIDE

Whiz quiz

Find out the name of the mascot of the Indian Railways.

30 Superhumans

Art and Entertainment

When there is chaos in the world, we need superhumans to save the planet.

Read the descriptions and match them to the names of some superhumans.

1. Peter Parker spins his webs across New York City and saves it from the clutches of Doctor Octopus.

2. Steve Rodgers becomes a super soldier, the leader of the Avengers.

3. Tony Stark is a genius and billionaire who, along with his virtual assistant, Edwin Jarvis, always saves the day.

4. Half-human and half-alien, Carol Danvers is one of the most powerful members of the Avengers. Thanks to her, the mighty Thanos was defeated.

5. The son of Odin and god of thunder, his hammer Mjolnir helps him win against his enemies.

a. Iron Man

b. Captain Marvel

c. Thor

d. Captain America

e. Spider-Man

Whiz fact

The Incredibles is a film series about superheroes who have been ordered not to use their superpowers, but are finally forced to use them to, what else, but save the world!

6 Billionaire Bruce Wayne becomes the Dark Knight to protect Gotham from the Joker.

7 Kal-El was born on the planet Krypton. He comes to Earth and becomes the Man of Steel.

8 Princess Diana uses her Lasso of Truth to tie up her enemies. She is the leader of the Amazons.

9 Barry Allen is the fastest man alive and uses his super speed to save Central City.

10 Arthur Curry is the King of the underwater kingdom Atlantis. He uses the Trident of Neptune to protect all the creatures of the sea.

11 Dr Robert Bruce Banner transforms into a huge, green-skinned humanoid possessing great strength.

f Aquaman

g Flash Gordon

h Batman

i Incredible Hulk

j Wonder Woman

k Superman

Whiz quiz

These superhumans are from two 'universes'—the Marvel Universe and the DC Universe. Can you say which characters are from which universe?

31 A Holiday in Australia

World Around Us

Read the clues and look at the map to find out some facts about Australia.

1 The city on the westernmost coast of Australia

.... E R ....

2 An island in the Southern Ocean which is a part of Australia

.... A S .... N .... A

3 The water body that separates Australia from an island to its south

.... A .... S S .... R .... T

4 The capital of Australia and its only major city not located on the coast

.... A N .... E R R ....

5 An animal native to Australia, it carries its baby in a pouch on its body.

.... A N G .... R ....

6 The world's largest structure built by living things, it can be seen from outer space.

.... R E .... T .... A R R .... R R .... F

7 The largest city of Australia, it is located on the east coast near the capital city.

.... Y D .... E ....

8 A large water body in northwest Australia

.... NDI .... CE .... N

9 An arrangement of stars on the flag of Australia which resembles a constellation

.... O U T .... E .... N C .... S S

10 A city famous for the largest cricket ground in Australia

.... E L .... O U ....

Whiz fact

The name Australia literally means 'Southern Land'. Its first official name was New Holland, which was given by the Dutch.

General Science

32 Space Odyssey

Read the descriptions and write the names of some space events and celestial objects using words from the help box.

1 A space event when the moon passes between the Earth and the Sun so that we cannot see all or part of the Sun for a time. ....

2 A piece of rock from outer space that makes a bright streak across the night sky as it burns up while falling through the Earth's atmosphere. ....

3 The star that is above the North Pole in the sky. It is the brightest star in the Ursa Major constellation.
....

4 A cloud of gas and dust in outer space that can be seen in the night sky either as an indistinct bright patch or a dark outline against a brighter background
....

5 The phase of moon during which it appears more than half but less than fully illuminated
....

Whiz quiz

What is the special building with a curved ceiling where we can see the stars and many other celestial bodies called?

....

6 A group of stars that form a pattern in the sky

....

7 The galaxy to which our solar system belongs

....

8 A rocky celestial object orbiting the Sun, though its size and orbit can vary. ....

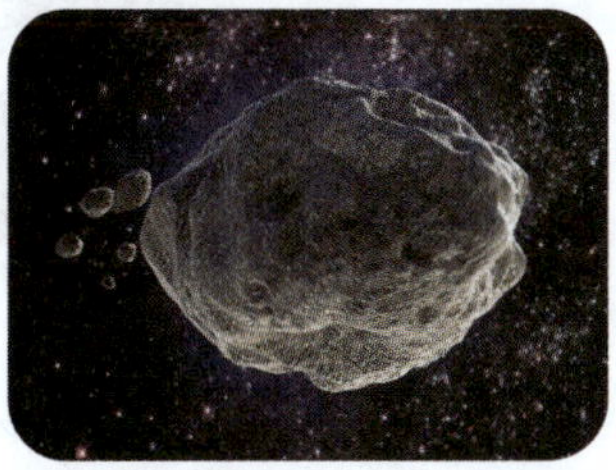

9 The Sun, the Earth, seven other planets, their moons and many other smaller celestial bodies together

....

10 A bright celestial object with a long tail that travels around the Sun ....

11 A dark patch or a spot that sometimes appears on the surface of the Sun ....

Help box

Nebula | Meteor | Sunspot | Constellation | Milky Way | Comet
Solar eclipse | North Star | Solar System | Gibbous | Asteroid

Whiz fact

The zodiac is an imaginary area in the sky in which the Sun, moon and planets appear to lie. The twelve signs of the zodiac have been named after constellations.

33 Grocery Shopping

INFORMATION

Let us go grocery shopping. Look at the pictures and write C for cereals, P for pulses, O for oilseeds and S for spices.

1 

Peanuts

....

2 

Wheat

....

3 

Turmeric

....

4 

Green gram

....

5 

Oats

....

6 

Cardamom

....

7 

Mustard

....

8 

Jowar

....

9 

Kidney beans

....

Whiz fact

The Spice Route was an ancient trade route followed by merchants, importers and exporters trading in exotic spices such as cloves and cinnamon.

34 Measuring Things

Read the paragraph and underline all the measuring words. Then write each measuring word in the correct column in the table given below.

Inch

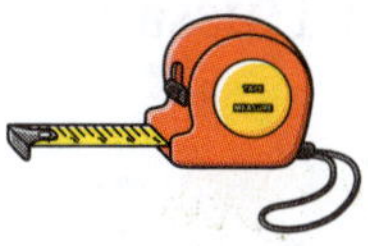

Metre

Litre

Kunal was not feeling well on Saturday. The next morning, his father took him to visit the doctor for a checkup. The doctor noted that he was 4 feet 1 inch tall and weighed 25 kilograms. He asked the nurse to give Kunal 0.5 millilitres of medicine. Then, Kunal and his father drove to the market and bought 3 kilograms of mangoes for Kunal's grandparents. After that, Kunal's father drove 20 kilometres to reach back home. It took them 2 hours because there was a lot of traffic. When they reached home, Kunal's grandfather gave him a 250 millilitres box of his favourite guava juice and a 50 grams packet of potato chips. Later in the evening, Kunal went with his grandmother to the market to buy new curtains for their 1-metre-wide window. Then in the night, they had dinner together. Kunal ate so much that when it was time for him to sleep, he fell asleep in 15 seconds.

Minute

Gram

Second

Time	Volume	Length/ Distance	Weight
....	....	....	....
....		....	....
		....	....
		....	

Whiz fact

Most countries around the world have now adopted the metric system. But in the United States and some other countries, distance is measured in miles, length is measured in feet, weight is measured in pounds and volume is measured in gallons. This is called the imperial system.

India Focus

35 Presidents of India

Here is how we can remember the names of all the Presidents of India in the correct order.

1 The first President of India took over from the British Raj.

Rajendra Prasad

2 The second President was the president of all—a part of his name, *Sarv* means 'all' in Sanskrit.

Sarvepalli Radhakrishnan

3 The third President shared his surname with the tabla maestro Zakir Hussain and the artist M F Hussain.

Zakir Hussain

4 There are four syllables in the fourth President's name—Vi-Vi-Gi-Ri.

V V Giri

5 The fifth President—F for Fakhruddin and F for five.

Fakhruddin Ali Ahmed

6 The sixth President was the Speaker of the Lok Sabha before he became the president.

Neelam Sanjiva Reddy

7 The seventh President was the first Sikh president of India.

Zail Singh

8 The eighth President of India has Lord Rama's name in his name.

R Venkataraman

9 Shankar is another name for Lord Shiva, the first name of the ninth President of India.

Shankar Dayal Sharma

10 The tenth President of India has the name of Lord Narayana in his name.

K R Narayanan

11 The eleventh President was renowned as the people's president and popular for his distinct hairstyle.

A P J Abdul Kalam

12 The twelfth President was the first woman President of India.

Pratibha Patil

13 The initials of the thirteenth President were PM, but he was the president.

Pranab Mukherjee

14 After a slew of Prime Ministers, the fourteenth President was India's first President from Uttar Pradesh!

Ram Nath Kovind

Answer these questions.

1. Who was the thirteenth President of India? ....
2. Who was the second President of India? ....
3. Who was the third President of India? ....
4. V V Giri was President number ....
5. Zail Singh was President number ....

Whiz fact

On 25 July 2022, Droupadi Murmu became the fifteenth President of India. She is the first tribal person and only the second woman to hold the President's office.

36 Safety First

A first aid kit is a box containing equipment needed to give immediate medical help in an emergency.

Tick (✓) the names of things from the first aid kit you will use in each of these emergency situations.

1. You sprained your ankle while running.
   - a sticking plaster
   - b crepe bandage
   - c antiseptic cream

2. You hid inside a bush while playing in the park and got red, itchy bumps on your legs.
   - a antiseptic cream
   - b skin-rash cream
   - c distilled water

3. A wooden splinter from a bench in the park got stuck in your friend's finger.
   - a tweezers
   - b scissors
   - c safety pins

4. A bee bit your ankle.
   - a antiseptic cream
   - b muscle relaxant
   - c insect-bite spray

5. A speck of dust has gotten into your eye.
   - a eye bath
   - b distilled water
   - c spectacle cleaner

6. You bruised your leg and want to clean it.
   - a painkillers
   - b distilled water
   - c antiseptic cream

7. You fell and hurt your forearm, and need to make a sling for it until you get to a doctor.
   - a sterile gauze pads
   - b adhesive tape
   - c bandage roll

Whiz fact

An expiry date of a medicine is the date from which it should not be used as it is no longer safe to be used or eaten. We should always remember to check expiry dates of medicines.

Learning Skills

37 Common Abbreviations

While writing, we use many short forms to save time and effort. These are called abbreviations. Several abbreviations are used in formal correspondence.

COMMUNICATION

Read this letter and write the full forms of the underlined abbreviations.

Dr Rishabh Bhatia
49A, Govind Street
Agra, UP 223007

Date: 14 November 2019

Subject: Parcel Containing Medical Equipment

Respected Sir,

With reference to your bill no. 52682, a parcel from Arizona, United States of America weighing 4.5 kg in a box measuring 30 × 34 × 6 cm has been dispatched at 15:00 hr and should reach you by 16 November 2019 before 18:00 hr. The equipment contained is worth $95 (approx. ₹6460; @ ₹79 = 1$), for which payment needs to be made.

Please pay using your credit card or e-wallet. You will receive an OTP by SMS for payment.

FYI, the box also contains a User Manual and a Warranty Card.

Regards,
Medical Equipment Association

1 ....
2 ....
3 ....
4 ....
5 ....
6 ....
7 ....
8 ....
9 ....
10 ....

Whiz fact

Many abbreviations in English are from foreign languages. PS stands for *post scriptum*, which is Latin for 'afterthought'. RSVP stands for *répondez s'il vous plaît,* which is French for 'please reply'.

13 CLIMATE ACTION

Climate Action

38 Biodegradable Things

Biodegradable things break down or decay naturally without causing pollution. Non-biodegradable things cause pollution as they do not decompose.

Look at the graph showing the amount of time it takes for things to biodegrade and read the statements below. Then write T for true and F for false in the box provided.

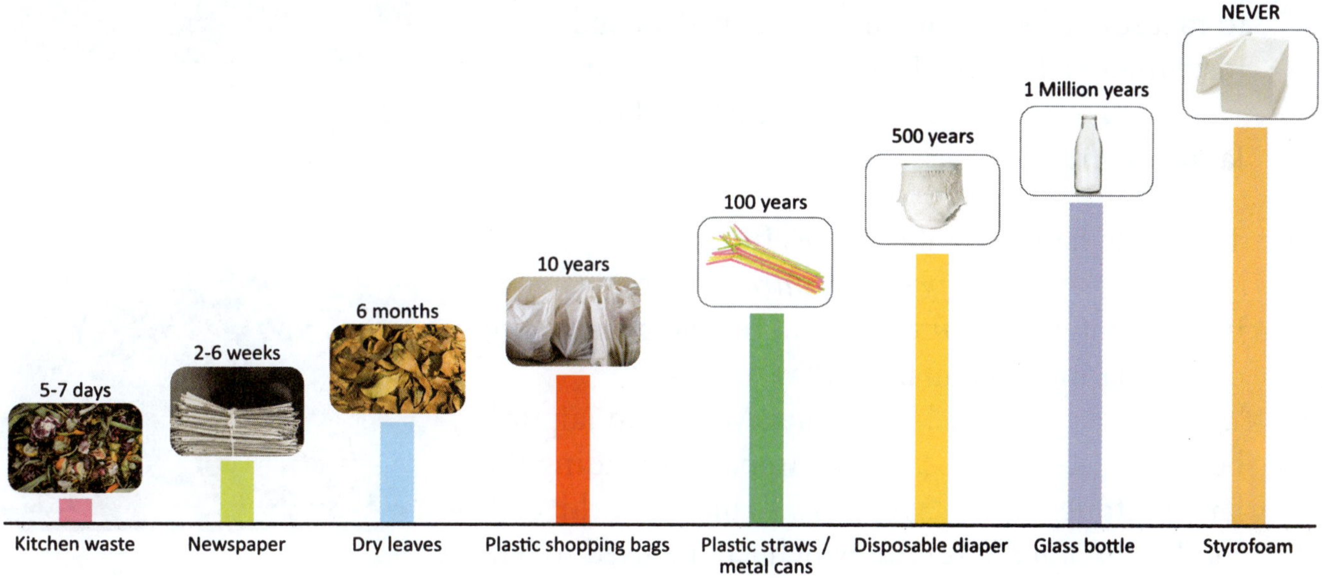

1. Styrofoam is non-biodegradable. ☐
2. It takes longer for plastic shopping bags to decompose than plastic straws. ☐
3. Disposable diapers are good for the environment. ☐
4. It is better to use newspaper than plastic as packaging material. ☐
5. Metal cans and plastic straws take same amount of time to biodegrade. ☐
6. Dry leaves take less time to decay naturally than kitchen waste. ☐
7. Metal cans and glass bottles are biodegradable. ☐
8. The time taken for the decomposition of disposable diaper is usually calculated in terms of days. ☐

Whiz fact

Plastic dumped into the sea is harmful for the sea creatures. Fish consume this plastic and die as they cannot digest it.

India Focus

39 Jantar Mantar

Read this text about the Jantar Mantar in Jaipur and fill in the blanks with words from the help box.

1 Sawai Jai Singh II was the founder of .... He was very interested in mathematics, science and astronomy. He wanted to measure time and distance using advanced instruments. In 1734, he commissioned a unique .... in Jaipur, which we know as Jantar Mantar.

2 The name Jantar Mantar comes from two .... words *yantra*, which means instrument, and *mantrana*, which means consulting or calculating. So Jantar Mantar means '......................................'. The Jantar Mantar in Jaipur has .... instruments, including the largest stone .... in the world, called the *Vrihat Samrat Yantra*, which can be used to tell the time accurately up to two seconds.

3 Other interesting instruments include the *Rashi Valaya Yantra*, a set of 12 dials that takes ecliptic measurements of the 12 .... constellations, the *Yantra Raj Yantra* that calculates the Hindu .... and the *Misra Yantra*, which is a mix of five different instruments.

4 The Jantar Mantar in Jaipur is a .... World Heritage Site.

Help box

Sanskrit | observatory | Jaipur | UNESCO | nineteen | zodiac | calculating instrument | calendar | sundial

Whiz fact

Sawai Jai Singh II commissioned and built five Jantar Mantars in all. Apart from the one in Jaipur, they were built in Delhi, Mathura, Ujjain and Varanasi.

Sports

40 Sporting Terms

Write the names of the sports with which these terms are associated.

1. backstroke butterfly freestyle lap

   ....

2. dismount vault balance beam floor exercise

   ....

3. shaft arrowhead arm guard target point

   ....

4. mat pin clamp hold

   ....

5. striker dribble drive flick

   ....

6. rough green fairway par

   ....

7. deuce set ace let

   ....

Whiz fact

Birdie, eagle and albatross are scores in golf. In the United States, the albatross is also called a double eagle.

41 State Capitals of India

Match these Indian states with their capitals with the help of the clues.

States	Clues	Capital Cities
1 Andhra Pradesh	The new capital	a Bengaluru
2 Arunachal Pradesh	The name of this city means 'brick and city'	b Shimla
3 Assam	A neighbourhood in Guwahati	c Ranchi
4 Bihar	The ancient city of Pataliputra	d Chandigarh
5 Chhattisgarh	The new version of an old city	e Thiruvananthapuram
6 Goa	Located on the banks of the river Mandovi	f Bhopal
7 Gujarat	Named after the Father of the Indian Nation	g Patna
8 Haryana	Capital of two states and a union territory	h Itanagar
9 Himachal Pradesh	The Queen of Hills	i Gandhinagar
10 Jharkhand	Named after the Oraon word for bamboo grove	j Dispur
11 Karnataka	The IT capital of India	k Amaravati
12 Kerala	The southernmost state capital on the Malabar Coast	l Nava Raipur
13 Madhya Pradesh	The 'City of Lakes'	m Panaji

	States	Clues		Capital Cities
14	Maharashtra	The financial capital of India	n	Dehradun
15	Manipur	The Kangla Place is located here	o	Agartala
16	Meghalaya	A beautiful city surrounded by the Khasi and the Garo hills	p	Bhubaneswar
17	Mizoram	The only capital city with the letter 'z' in its name	q	Hyderabad
18	Nagaland	The name of this city means 'the land of the kewhi flower'	r	Chennai
19	Odisha	This city replaced Cuttack as the capital 1948	s	Shillong
20	Punjab	Also the capital city of Haryana	t	Kolkata
21	Rajasthan	The Pink City	u	Lucknow
22	Sikkim	The name of this city means 'hill top'	v	Chandigarh
23	Tamil Nadu	Formerly known as Madras	w	Kohima
24	Telangana	Charminar is located in this city	x	Aizawl
25	Tripura	Named after Agarwood trees	y	Imphal
26	Uttar Pradesh	The ancient princely state of Awadh	z	Jaipur
27	Uttarakhand	Combination of two words: *dera* and *dun*	aa	Mumbai
28	West Bengal	The capital of India until 1911, formerly known as Calcutta	bb	Gangtok

Learning Skills

42 Brain Teasers

CRITICAL THINKING

Here are twelve brain teasers. Try to solve five in two minutes. Then, try to solve the other seven. Your time starts now!

1. In a single-storey orange house, everything was orange—an orange person, an orange cat, an orange fish, an orange computer, an orange chair, an orange table, an orange telephone and an orange shower. What colour were the stairs?

   ....

2. Arti's mother had three children. The first one was Pratham and the second one was Dwitiya. What was the name of the third child?

   ....

3. Two ducks in front of a duck, two ducks behind a duck. One duck each in front and behind a duck. How many ducks in total?

   ....

4. Which weighs more—a kilo of bricks or a kilo of feathers?

   ....

5. How many months have 28 days?

   ....

Whiz quiz

Make two brain teasers on your own.

....

....

....

6 You are running a race. You run past the person at the second position. At what position are you running now?

7 If you keep one candy in a magic box, it turns into two candies in one minute. In another one minute, two candies double to four candies. If the magic box is full of candy in fifteen minutes, how much candy did it have at the end of fourteen minutes?

8 There are eight apples and you take away two. How many apples will you have?

9 Imagine you are in a room filling with water. There are no windows or doors. How do you get out?

10 You are in a room at night and it is absolutely dark. You have one matchstick. Which one of these would you light first—the newspaper, the lamp, the candle or the fire?

11 What appears once in a minute, twice in a moment, but never in a thousand years?

12 What travels faster: heat or cold?

Language and Literature

43 Which Book is That?

Read the clues and select the correct words to complete the names of these books. Match the authors to the books by writing the correct letters in the boxes.

1 Every night, Charlie listens to Grandpa Joe tell stories about Mr Willy Wonka. ☐

Charlie and the .... Soap/Chocolate Factory

2 Jerusha Abbott was brought up at an old-fashioned orphanage. The children were wholly dependent on charity. ☐

Daddy-Long .... -Legs/Hair

3 Two young children, Sally and Sam, are having a very dull day. Their mother is out and then the Cat comes in. ☐

The Cat in the .... Hat/Hut

4 Laura and her family live in a log cabin in the woods of Wisconsin. ☐

Little/Big .... House on the Prairie

5 Young Binya falls in love with a gorgeous umbrella owned by a Japanese tourist. ☐

The .... Pink/Blue Umbrella

6 Young Max is naughty and mischievous and not afraid of anything. ☐

Where the .... Wild/Beautiful Things Are

7 Ramona Quimby is no longer seven, but not quite eight, not allowed to stay home alone, yet old enough to watch pesky Willa Jean.

Ramona and her .... *Mother/Teacher*

8 Mischievous Fudge repeatedly gets into trouble. He refuses to eat for four days and swallows his brother Peter's pet turtle.

Tales of A Fourth Grade .... *Something/Nothing*

9 Matthew Cuthbert and Marilla Cuthbert are siblings who live on their ancestral farm in the quiet town of Avonlea in Prince Edward Island, Canada.

Anne/Jane .... *of Green Gables*

10 One day Lucy finds a wardrobe that transports her to a magical world.

The .... *Tiger/Lion, The* ....

Ghost/Witch, and The Wardrobe

a 
Beverly Cleary

b 
Dr Seuss

c 
C S Lewis

d 
Lucy Maud Montgomery

e 
Roald Dahl

f 
Judy Blume

g 
Laura Ingalls Wilder

h 
Jean Webster

i 
Ruskin Bond

j 
Maurice Sendak

Whiz fact

Christopher Robin was the name of A A Milne's son. The stories he wrote were inspired by his son's stuffed animals, especially his teddy bear.

India Focus

44 Param Vir Chakra

The Param Vir Chakra is awarded for most conspicuous bravery or some daring or pre-eminent act of valour or self-sacrifice, in the presence of the enemy, whether on land, at sea or in the air. Officers of all ranks from the Navy, the Military and the Air Force are eligible for this gallantry award.

Look at the images of the Param Vir Chakra medal and choose the correct answers.

Front Back

1 The Param Vir Chakra medal is made of bronze/silver.

2 The medal has the flag/emblem of India in the centre.

3 The medal has four replicas of Indra's Vajra/Vishnu's Sudarshan on the front.

4 The back of the medal has the words Param Vir Chakra written in Sanskrit and Tamil/Hindi and English.

5 The flower on the back of the medal is a lotus/rose.

6 The medal is suspended from a black/purple ribbon.

Whiz fact

The Param Vir Chakra is conferred by the President of India. A record of persons who have been awarded the Param Vir Chakra is kept in a public journal called *The Gazette of India*.

Sports

45 Equipped to Play

Every sport needs special equipment.

Find the names of sports equipment hidden in this word grid and write their names.

I	T	Y	L	E	F	G	C	S	F	C
R	B	O	A	R	D	H	L	P	R	L
O	S	T	A	R	M	H	U	E	I	U
S	U	R	F	B	O	A	R	D	N	B
C	L	E	A	T	S	D	D	L	G	E
L	G	F	O	R	E	I	G	N	D	Y
A	L	D	B	A	R	B	E	L	L	S
M	O	R	P	L	A	S	T	I	C	K
P	V	O	B	G	B	E	W	C	H	A
I	E	N	E	R	A	C	Q	U	E	T
S	S	E	N	F	T	C	O	E	Z	E
R	A	G	J	O	W	F	R	T	A	S

1. Squash ....
2. Golf ....
3. Baseball ....
4. Weightlifting ....
5. Boxing ....
6. Surfing ....
7. Ice skating ....
8. Snooker ....

Whiz fact

In the book *Alice's Adventures in Wonderland*, the Queen invites Alice to play a very strange game of croquet. The equipment used are live hedgehogs in place of croquet balls, and flamingos as mallets.

India

Focus

46 Percussion Instruments

Percussion instruments make a sound when they are struck, shaken or scraped. They usually add rhythm or beat to music.

Read the clues and write the names of some percussion instruments of India using picture clues.

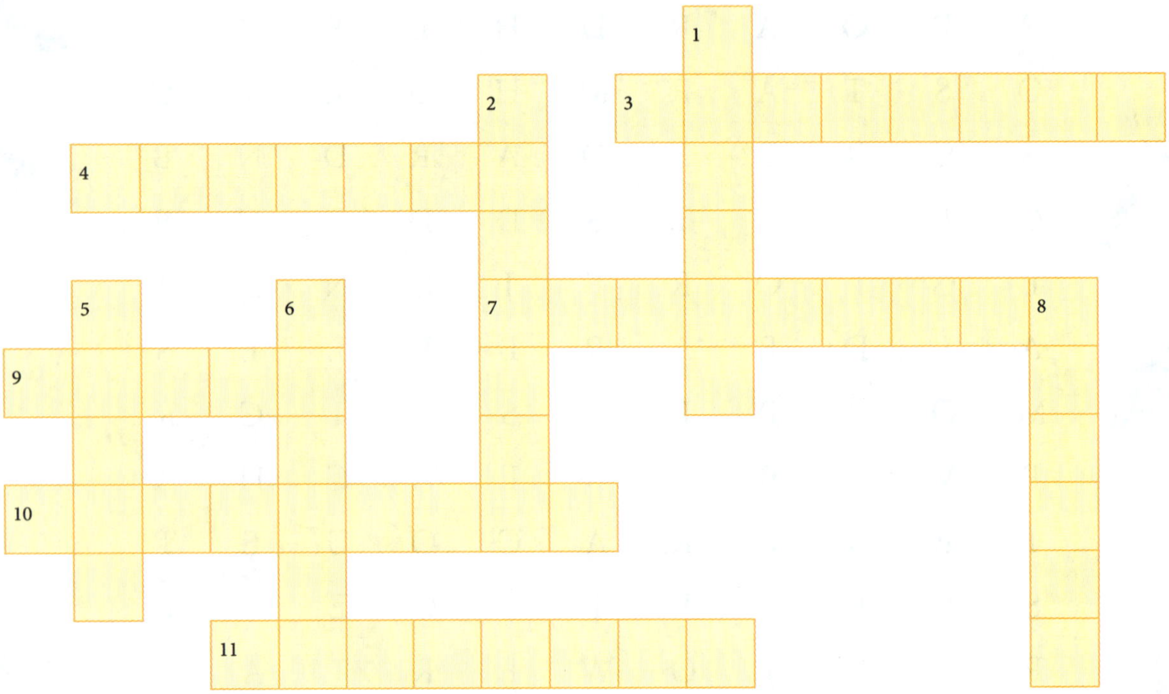

Across

3 Small metallic bells strung together, often worn as anklets

4 A South Indian folk and bhajan frame drum of the tambourine family

7 Ceramic or metal bowls tuned with water and played by striking the edges with beaters

9 Two single-headed, barrel-shaped small drums with a playing technique involving extensive use of the fingers and palms

10 Wooden double-headed drum from South India believed to have been split into two to create a popular north Indian percussion instrument

11 A barrel-shaped, two-headed drum with a low, mellow tone; it is tuned with the help of wooden wedges and ropes

Down

1. A tongs with small brass jingles or rings
2. A pair of small hand-clash cymbals
5. A small two-headed drum known as the instrument of Lord Shiva
6. A bowl-shaped drum, typically played with a pair of sticks during traditional ceremonies
8. A clay pot with a narrow mouth

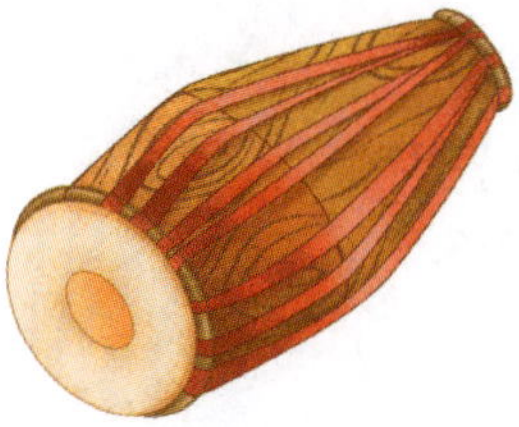

Mridangam

Chimta

Jal tarang

Kanjira

Ghatam

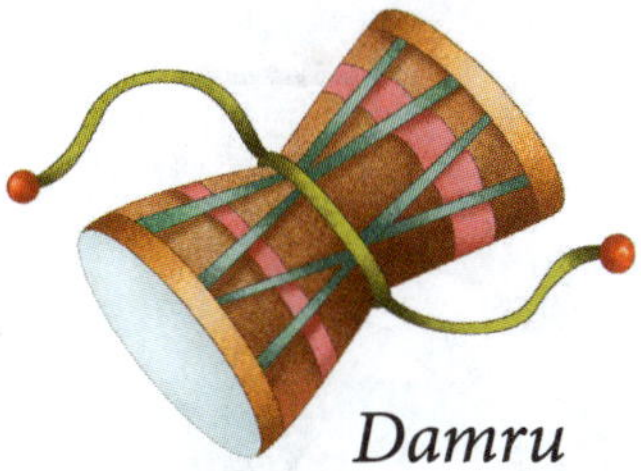

Damru

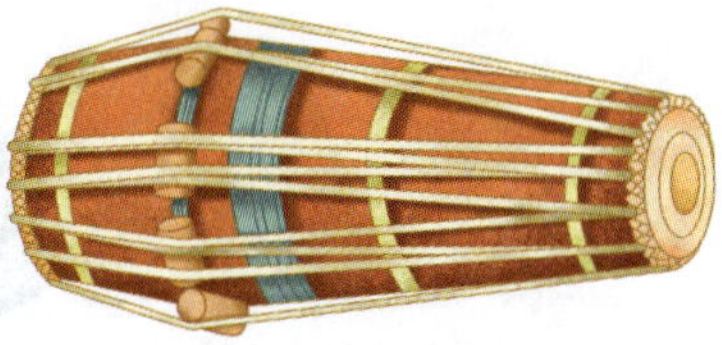

Pakhavaj

Ghungroo

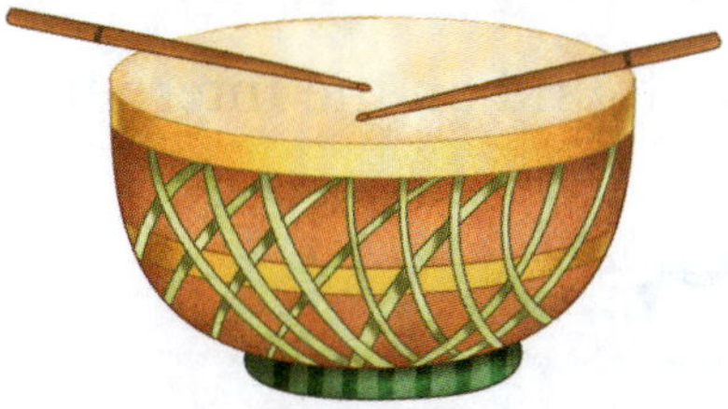

Nagara

Tabla

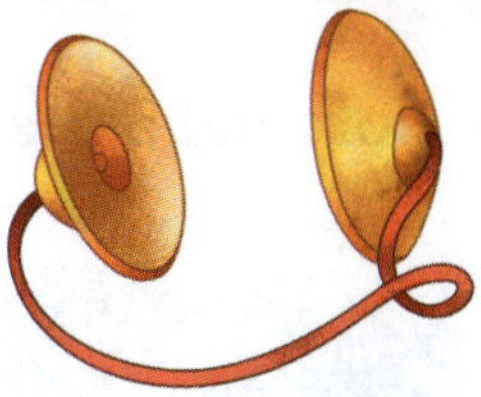

Manjira

Whiz fact

The *dholak* is a two-headed hand drum. It is a folk instrument that does not have exact tuning. It is related to the bigger dhol and the smaller *dholki*.

47 Getting Things Done

Life Skills

We should plan our work-time and study-time wisely to have time for fun and recreation. We can complete a task efficiently by breaking it into small steps.

PROBLEM SOLVING

Here is a project assigned to you. Arrange these pictures in the correct order so that you can complete your project in time.

Project

Prepare a short report on geography, wildlife, people and culture of any one state of India. Draw or paste pictures to show and explain things you have written about. You can base your research on the following points.

Geography: Mountains, rivers, seas and lands

Wildlife: Birds and animals found in any one state

People and culture: Languages, festivals, food habits and clothing of the people

1 

Write the report and paste pictures.

2 

Print pictures found on the Internet.

3 

Make a cover page for the report.

4 

Buy paper, glue and any other materials needed.

5

Make a to-do list of tasks.

6

Find information on the Internet and in books.

7

Make a list of pictures needed.

8

Make timelines for each task in the to-do list.

Whiz quiz

Which of these actions will you do to plan your daily routine?

a Make a schedule b Overthink c Do things randomly

Whiz fact

Huge tasks such as building dams, bridges and metro lines take years to complete. A large number of people and materials are needed to make such projects successful. The way in which these tasks can be done is called project management.

India Focus

48 Wildlife of Northeast India

Northeast India has many species of birds and animals that are not found elsewhere in India.

Fill in the blanks with the correct answers.

1 The .... snow leopard/clouded leopard is the state animal of Meghalaya.

2 The .... gibbon/serow is the state animal of Mizoram.

3 The gaur or .... Indian/Malaysian bison is the state animal of Nagaland.

4 The .... Purple Panda/Red Panda is the state animal of Sikkim.

5 The Phayre's langur or leaf .... monkey/bear is the state animal of Tripura.

6 The .... gayal/crocodile is the state animal of Arunachal Pradesh.

7 The one-horned .... buffalo/rhino is the state animal of Assam.

8 The Sangai or brow-antlered .... boar/deer is the state animal of Manipur.

9 Mizoram and Manipur share the same state bird, the male Mrs Hume's pheasant. It has a long blue and .... yellow/black and brown tail.

10 The white-winged wood duck is the state bird of Assam and has black patterns on its .... white/orange head and neck.

11 The state bird of Arunachal Pradesh, the great hornbill, is notable for its black and yellow .... helmet-like/wing-like projection over its large bill.

12 The hill myna with its glossy green-black plumage and bright .... yellow-orange/blue-green patches is the state bird of Meghalaya.

13 The state bird of Nagaland is Blyth's tragopan, a vulnerable species of pheasant with a grey belly and a .... rusty red/bottle green head.

14 The blood pheasant is the state bird of Sikkim. It has .... white/dark grey feathers.

49 Word Relationships

Let us look at some word relationships. The words to the left of the proportion sign (: :) are related in the same way as the words to the right of it. Such relationships are called analogies.

CRITICAL THINKING

Choose the correct words to make correct word relationships.

1. FINGER : HAND : : .... : FOOT

   a Ankle b Toes c Toe d Heel

2. YAWN : .... : : SMILE : HAPPINESS

   a Sleep b Teeth c Sadness d Tiredness

3. .... : BOTTOM : : UP : DOWN

   a Below b Top c Above d Upstairs

4. ANKLET : ANKLE : : BRACELET : ....

   a Arm b Elbow c Brace d Wrist

5. DAY : WEEK : : .... : YEAR

   a Hour b Second c Month d Century

6. WOMAN : .... : : GIRL : BOY

   a Man b Person c Husband d Brother

7. CHATTER : MONKEY : : CLUCK : ....

   a Horse b Hen c Hippopotamus d Hamster

8. .... : PLAY : : BED : SLEEP

   a Park b Chess c Player d Football

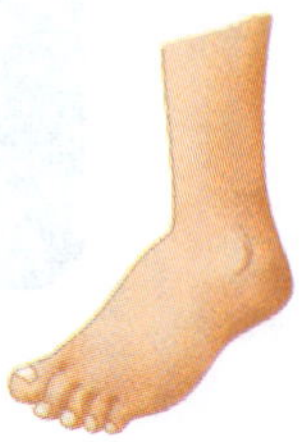

March						
				1	2	3
4	5	6	7	8	9	10
11	12	13	14	15	16	17
18	19	20	21	22	23	24
25	26	27	28	29	30	31

Quiz Yourself 1

Fill in the blanks with the correct answers.

1. The state animal of Assam is the ....
   (a) one-horned rhino (b) tiger
   (c) mithun (d) black bear
2. Clubs are used in the sport of ....
   (a) hockey (b) golf
   (c) lacrosse (d) Fencing
3. The .... valley in Ladakh is popular for trekking.
   (a) Barak (b) Chamba
   (c) Zanskar (d) Doon
4. A .... shaped road sign is used as a sign of warning.
   (a) triangular (b) square
   (c) circular (d) rectangular
5. A .... is a word that reads the same forwards and backwards.
   (a) anagram (b) homophone
   (c) antonym (d) palindrome
6. A male goose is called a ....
   (a) drake (b) gander
   (c) tom (d) rooster
7. The .... mountains are also known as the Blue Mountains.
   (a) Vindhya (b) Sahyadri
   (c) Nilgiri (d) Aravalli
8. A .... is an instrument doctors use for measuring body temperature.
   (a) Micrometer (b) Ammeter
   (c) Barometer (d) Thermometer
9. A .... could take a million years to degrade.
   (a) rubber tyre (b) cotton t-shirt
   (c) metal can (d) glass bottle
10. The festival of .... marks the end of winter in Punjab.
   (a) Baisakhi (b) Holi
   (c) Lohri (d) Shivratri

Quiz Yourself 2

Fill in the blanks with the correct answers.

1. The Black Diamond Express runs from Kolkata to ...., a town where coal mines are found.
   (a) Dhanbad (b) Neyveli
   (c) Talcher (d) Jamshedpur
2. The only new Indian currency note which does not have a monument depicted on it, is the Rs .... note.
   (a) 100 (b) 200 (c) 500 (d) 2000
3. Distance is still measured using miles, and not kilometres, in ....
   (a) India (b) UK
   (c) USA (d) Japan
4. The .... is a bird of prey with powerful talons and keen eyesight.
   (a) Pigeon (b) Kite
   (c) Ostrich (d) Hummingbird
5. '*Satyamev Jayate*' literally translates to ....
   (a) always tell the truth (b) truth is victory
   (c) truth alone triumphs (d) there is only one truthc
6. Kolkata is also called the ....
   (a) City of Dreams (b) City of Light
   (c) City of Joy (d) City of Lakes
7. The app that has a little blue bird with a pointy beak. ....
   (a) Twitter (b) Snapchat (c) Google Chrome (d) YouTube
8. The brightest star in the .... constellation is the North Star or the Pole Star.
   (a) Ursa Minor (b) Orion
   (c) Ursa Major (d) Cassiopeia
9. The .... is a sea creature with eight limbs that can walk on the ocean floor.
   (a) seahorse (b) sea anemone
   (c) starfish (d) octopus
10. The .... is a wraparound Japanese dress worn with a sash.
    (a) koneko (b) kimono
    (c) kabuki (d) kujaku

Quiz Yourself 3

Fill in the blanks with the correct answers.

1. The French word for 'tag' or 'label' is ....
   (a) couture (b) labelle
   (c) etiquette (d) ravissant
2. L, C, D and M are .... numerals.
   (a) Arabic (b) Roman
   (c) Hindu (d) Greek
3. .... was the first person to manufacture automobiles on a mass scale in a factory using the 'assembly line' system of manufacturing.
   (a) James Watt (b) Henry Ford
   (c) Thomas Edison (d) Karl Benz
4. The .... is a big cat which is more at home on trees than on the ground, and has the longest canine teeth of any living feline.
   (a) clouded leopard (b) snow leopard
   (c) cheetah (d) panther
5. The .... is the short form for a special dress worn by health workers especially during the COVID-19 pandemic.
   (a) WHO (b) CVC
   (c) PPF (d) PPE
6. Mohammad Iqbal composed ....
   (a) *Sare Jahan Se Accha* (b) *Jana Gana Mana*
   (c) *Vande Mataram* (d) *Amar Sonar Bangla*
7. In the Harry Potter series of books, Mr. and Mrs. Dursley lived at ....
   (a) 221B Baker Street (b) Number 4, Privet Drive
   (c) No. 12 Grimmauld Place (d) Ottery St. Catchpole
8. The .... is the most important bird in Chinese legend.
   (a) Hippogriff (b) Gryphon
   (c) Phoenix (d) Roc
9. The city on the westernmost coast of Australia is ....
   (a) Sydney (b) Melbourne
   (c) Perth (d) Brisbane
10. The .... range is one of the oldest mountain ranges in the world.
   (a) Khasi (b) Aravalli (c) Satpura (d) Pir Panjal

Quiz Yourself 4

Fill in the blanks with the correct answers.

1. A list of special words and their meanings in a book is called a/an ....
   (a) Glossary (b) Index
   (c) Preface (d) Epilogue
2. 'Super Man Helps Every One' is a mnemonic to help remember the ....
   (a) five senses (b) five Great Lakes
   (c) five oceans (d) five rivers of Punjab
3. Peter Parker is the alter-ego of ....
   (a) Batman (b) Superman
   (c) Ironman (d) Spiderman
4. The now-extinct .... was a half-zebra and half-horse.
   (a) Dodo (b) Great Auk
   (c) Quagga (d) Pyrenean ibex
5. The festival of .... celebrated in April, marks the new year in Kerala.
   (a) Bihu (b) Vishu
   (c) Ugadi (d) Gudi Padwa
6. .... is a small aquatic plant with white flowers whose leaves are eaten raw in salads.
   (a) buttonbush (b) lizard's tail
   (c) Japanese iris (d) water cress
7. .... is the largest of the four principal islands of Japan.
   (a) Shikoku (b) Honshu
   (c) Kyushu (d) Hokkaido
8. The Great .... runs several thousand kilometres and is considered a man-made wonder of the world.
   (a) Wall of China (b) Pyramid at Giza
   (c) Barrier Reef (d) Pyramid of the Sun
9. The logo of the .... is a set of 4 rings.
   (a) Olympic Games (b) Fiat
   (c) Audi (d) Commonwealth Games
10. *Inquilab Zindabad* is a line associated most closely with ....
    (a) Netaji Subhas Chandra Bose (b) Bankim Chandra Chattopadhyaya
    (c) Lal Bahadur Shastri (d) Shahid Bhagat Singh

Answer Key

Page 9: 1. Pink City; 2. Blue City; 3. Blue Mountains; 4. yellow; 5. Black Diamond Express; 6. Red Fort

Page 10-11: 1. kite; 2. pelican; 3. crane; 4. bulbul; 5. frogmouth; 6. darter; 7. condor; 8. emu

Page 12: Across: 4. syringe; 5. thermometer; 7. injection; 8. antiseptic

Down: 1. bandage; 2. chemist; 3. stethoscope; 6. pill

Page 13: 1. mom; 2. noon; 3. rotor; 4. kayak; 5. level; 6. wow

Page 14: 1. fish; 2. penguin; 3. sea turtle; 4. frog; 5. octopus; 6. jellyfish; 7. snake; 8. stingray

Page 15: 1. Jenny; 2. Boar; 3. Hen, Rooster; 4. Cow; 5. Buck; 6. Vixen, Dog; 7. Goose, Gander; 8. Billy; 9. Stallion; 10. Ewe, Ram; 11. Pen; 12. Queen

Page 16-17: m: Across: 2. cheetah; 4. jaguar; 6. snow leopard; 8. leopard

Down: 1. puma; 2. clouded leopard; 3. tiger; 5. lion; 7. lynx

Page 18-19: 2. d iii; 3. a iv; 4. b i; 5. h vii; 6. g v; 7. f viii; 8. e vi

Page 20-21:

2. Notes: ₹500, ₹50, ₹20 Coins: ₹2;

3. Notes: ₹500, ₹100, ₹200 Coins: 0;

4. Notes: ₹2000, ₹500 Coins: 0;

5. Notes: ₹20 Coins: ₹2;

6. Notes: ₹2000, ₹100, ₹10 Coins: 0

Page 22: Across: 2. Quarantine; 5. China; 6. Mask; 8. PPE; 11. Coronavirus; 13. India

Down: 1. Virus; 3. USA; 4. WHO; 7. Antibody; 9. Pandemic; 10. Covaxin; 12. Swab

Page 23: 1. No left turn; 2. Airport ahead; 3. Speed breaker ahead; 4. Zebra crossing; 5. No U turn; 6. Directions; 7. Narrow road ahead; 8. Pedestrian crossing prohibited

Page 24-25: 1. noodles; 2. Dragon; 3. compass; 4. cheongsam; 5. tea; 6. sky lantern; 7. chopsticks; 8. Lantern Festival; 9. Chinese Phoenix; 10. Great Wall of China; 11. Mandarin; 12. lotus

Page 26-27: 1. Bhai dooj; 2. Vishu; 3. Eid ul-Fitr; 4. Khordad Sal; 5. Rath Yatra; 6. Janamashtami; 7. Gurpurab; 8. Ugadi; 9. Mahavir Jayanti; 10. Milad-un-Nabi; 11. Christmas; 12. Lohri; 13. Herath

Page 28-29: 1. planets; 2. Great Lakes; 3. Roman numerals; 4. Central America; 5. Canada; 6. European; 7. Adriatic Sea

Page 30-31: 1. d; 2. a; 3. e; 4. c; 5. b; 6. j; 7. i; 8. f; 9. h; 10. g

Page 32: 1. *Hind*; 2. *Jayate*; 3. *Zindabad*; 4. *Mataram*; 5. *Kisaan*

Page 33: 1. f, ✓; 2. e, ✗; 3. d. ✓; 4. c, ✗; 5. b, ✗; 6. a, ✗

Page 34-35: 1. ; 2. 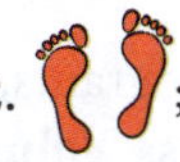; 3. 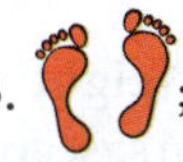; 4. ; 5. 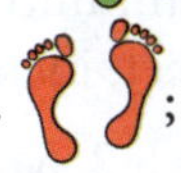; 6. 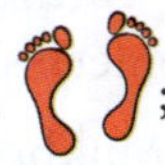; 7. ; 8. 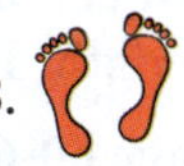

Page 36: 1. Bengali, Rabindranath Tagore; 2. 52; 3. Muhammad Iqbal, Urdu; 4. Pandit Ravi Shankar, *Taranah-e-Hindi*; 5. Bankim Chandra Chattopadhyay, Anandamath; 6. 1937

Page 37: 1. *Madeline*; 2. *Diary of a Wimpy Kid*; 3. *The Wizard of Oz*; 4. *Matilda*; 5. *Cat in the Hat*; 6. *Harry Potter and the Philosopher's Stone*; 7. *The Lightening Thief*

Page 38-39: 1. c; 2. e; 3. b; 4. f; 5. d; 6. a; 7. h; 8. j; 9. k; 10. m; 11. l; 12. g; 13. i

Page 40: 1. Borneo, Sumatra; 2. Honshu; 3. Jamaica; 4. Madagascar; 5. Ireland; 6. Sri Lanka; 7. Cyprus; 8. Taiwan

Page 41: 1. Snapchat; 2. Clubhouse; 3. Google Chrome; 4. Twitter; 5. Google Maps; 6. YouTube

Page 42-43: 1. Punjab; 2. Himachal Pradesh; 3. Uttarakhand; 4. Himachal Pradesh; 5. Uttar Pradesh; 6. Jammu and Kashmir; 7. Uttar Pradesh; 8. Himachal Pradesh; 9. Ladakh; 10. Punjab

Page 44-45: 1. Q, U; 2. M; 3. B, H; 4. X, I, Z; 5. S, P, N; 6. L, C; 7. V, T; 8. G; 9. D; 10. W, Y, A, O; 11. R, K; 12. J, E, F

Page 46-47: 1. Himalayas; 2. Western Ghats, Eastern Ghats; 3. Vindhya Range; 4. Garo Hills and Khasi Hills; 5. Aravalli Range

Page 48: Across: 3. glossary; 5. index; 6. preface

Down: 1. chapter; 2. flyleaf; 4. spine

Page 49: 1. f; 2. h; 3. g; 4. e; 5. a; 6. b; 7. c; 8. d

Page 50-51: a. 9; b. 4; c. 5; d. 2; e. 6; f. 8; g. 1; h. 7; i. 10; j. 3

Page 52-53: 1. e; 2. d; 3. a; 4. b; 5. c; 6. h; 7. k; 8. j; 9. g; 10. f; 11. i

Page 54-55: 1. Perth; 2. Tasmania; 3. Bass Strait; 4. Canberra; 5. Kangaroo; 6. Great Barrier Reef; 7. Sydney; 8. Indian Ocean; 9. Southern Cross; 10. Melbourne

Page 56-57: 1. Solar eclipse; 2. Meteor; 3. North Star; 4. Nebula; 5. Gibbous; 6. Constellation; 7. Milky Way; 8. Asteroid; 9. Solar System; 10. Comet; 11. Sunspot

Page 58: 1. O; 2. C; 3. S; 4. P; 5. C; 6. S; 7. O; 8. C; 9. P

Page 59: Weight: kilograms, kilograms, grams; **Time:** hours, seconds; **Volume:** millilitres; **Length/ Distance:** kilometres; feet, inch, metre

Page 60-61: 1. Pranab Mukherjee; 2. Sarvepalli Radhakrishnan; 3. Zakir Hussain; 4. four; 5. seven

Page 62-63: 1. b; 2. b; 3. a; 4. c; 5. a; 6. b; 7. c

Page 64: 1. doctor; 2. Uttar Pradesh; 3. number; 4. kilograms; 5. centimetres; 6. hours; 7. approximately; 8. One Time Password; 9. Short Messaging Service; 10. For Your Information

Page 65: 1. T; 2. F; 3. F; 4. T; 5. T; 6. F; 7. T; 8. F

Page 66: 1. Jaipur, observatory; 2. Sanskrit, calculating instrument, nineteen, sundial; 3. zodiac, calendar; 4. UNESCO

Page 67: 1. swimming; 2. gymnastics; 3. archery; 4. wrestling; 5. hockey; 6. golf; 7. tennis

Page 68-69: 1. k; 2. h; 3. j; 4. g; 5. l; 6. m; 7. i; 8. d; 9. b; 10. c; 11. a; 12. e; 13. f; 14. aa; 15. y; 16. s; 17. x; 18. w; 19. p; 20. v; 21. z; 22. bb; 23. r; 24. q; 25. o; 26. u; 27. n; 28. t

Page 70-71: 1. There are no stairs in a single-storey house; 2. Arti; 3. three; 4. both have the same weight; 5. 12; 6. second; 7. 28; 8. 2; 9. You cannot get in if there are no doors and windows; 10. fire; 11. the letter M; 12. heat travels faster, you can catch cold

Page 72-73: 1. *Chocolate*, e; 2. *Legs*, h; 3. *Hat*, b; 4. *Little*, g; 5. *Blue*, i; 6. *Wild*, j; 7. *Mother*, a; 8. *Nothing*, f; 9. *Anne*, d; 10. *Lion*, *Witch*, c

Page 74: 1. bronze; 2. emblem; 3. Indra's Vajra; 4. Hindi; 5. lotus; 6. purple

Page 75:

I	T	Y	L	E	F	G	C	S	F	C
R	B	O	A	R	D	H	L	P	R	L
O	S	T	A	R	M	H	U	E	I	U
S	U	R	F	B	O	A	R	D	N	B
C	L	E	A	T	S	D	D	L	G	E
L	G	F	O	R	E	I	G	N	D	Y
A	L	D	B	A	R	B	E	L	L	S
M	O	R	P	L	A	S	T	I	C	K
P	V	O	B	G	B	E	W	C	H	A
I	E	N	E	R	A	C	Q	U	E	T
S	S	E	N	F	T	C	O	E	Z	E
R	A	G	J	O	W	F	R	T	A	S

1. racquet; 2. club; 3. bat; 4. barbells; 5. gloves; 6. surfboard; 7. skates; 8. cue

Page 76-77: Across: 3. ghungroo; 4. kanjira; 7. jal tarang; 9. tabla; 10. mridangam; 11. pakhavaj

Down: 1. manjira; 2. chimta; 5. damru; 6. nagara; 8. ghatam

Page 78-79: 1. 7; 2. 5; 3. 8; 4. 6; 5. 1; 6. 3; 7. 4; 8. 2

Page 80-81: 1. clouded leopard; 2. serow; 3. Indian; 4. Red Panda; 5. monkey; 6. gayal; 7. rhino; 8. deer; 9. black and brown; 10. white; 11. helmet-like; 12. yellow-orange; 13. rusty red; 14. dark grey

Page 82: 1. Toe; 2. Sleep; 3. Top; 4. Wrist; 5. Month; 6. Man; 7. Hen; 8. Park

Page 83: Quiz Yourself 1: 1. a; 2. b; 3. c; 4. a; 5. d; 6. b; 7. c; 8. d; 9. d; 10. c

Page 84: Quiz Yourself 2: 1. a; 2. d; 3. c; 4. b; 5. c; 6. c; 7. a; 8. c; 9. d; 10. b

Page 85: Quiz Yourself 3: 1. c; 2. b; 3. b; 4. a; 5. d; 6. a; 7. b; 8. c; 9. c; 10. b

Page 86: Quiz Yourself 4: 1. a; 2. b; 3. d; 4. c; 5. b; 6. d; 7. b; 8. a; 9. c; 10. d